Two week
loan

MANAGING MANAGEMENT
PMENT

Please return on or before the last
date stamped below.
Charges are made for late return.

IS 239/0799

MANAGING WORK AND ORGANIZATIONS SERIES

Edited by Dr Graeme Salaman, Professor of Organisation Studies in the Faculty of Social Sciences and the Open Business School, the Open University

Current titles:

MANAGING MANAGEMENT DEVELOPMENT

Graham Mole

Open University Press
Buckingham · Philadelphia

Open University Press
Celtic Court
22 Ballmoor
Buckingham
MK18 1XW

email: enquiries@openup.co.uk
world wide web: www.openup.co.uk

and 325 Chestnut Street
Philadelphia, PA 19106, USA

First Published 2000

A catalogue record of this book is available from the British Library

ISBN   0 335 20134 2 (pb)   0 335 20135 0 (hb)

Library of Congress Cataloging-in-Publication Data
Mole, Graham, 1949–
    Managing management development / Graham Mole.
        p. cm – (Managing work and organizations series)
    Includes bibliographical references and index.
    ISBN 0-335-20135-0 – ISBN 0-335-20134-2 (pbk.)
    1. Executives – Training of – Great Britain.   2. Executives – Training
of – United States.   3. Management – Study and teaching – Great
Britain.   4. Management – Study and teaching – United States.
5. Organizational behavior – Great Britain.   6. Organizational
behavior – United States.   I. Title.   II. Series.

HD30.42.G7. M65 2000
658.4'07124–dc21   99-088205

Typeset by Type Study, Scarborough
Printed in Great Britain by The Cromwell Press, Trowbridge

For Lyz

This also acknowledges the help of those managers whom I remember as being particularly developmental in the early part of my career. From my days at Unilever, I recall especially Hywel David, Alec MacMillan and Joe Parkinson, from Anglo-American, John Godsall and Tony Paradine, and from Willis Faber and Dumas (as it then was), David Smith, Frank Walker and Lynda Woodman. It is a sobering and humbling thought that if organizations employed a few more people like them, they would need far fewer people like me.

GWM

CONTENTS

INTRODUCTION

Anyone who decides to critically examine the subject of management development encounters an early difficulty. If it is a researchable phenomenon then it is an extremely broad and amorphous one. It has become a portmanteau term which can be used to cover and justify a multitude of activities concerned with influencing the effectiveness of those who perform, or are about to perform, or aspire one day to perform, an organizational role which carries the label of 'management'. So management development, as popularly interpreted, could mean something as long-term as an educational programme such as a Master in Business Administration degree, or something as short as reading a journal or newspaper article about almost any aspect of organizational life. It can be applied at all four of the levels of analysis which social scientists are wont to apply to phenomena: individual, such as one person attending a training event; group, such as team training; organizational, such as preparing managers for the implementation of a corporate 'change programme'; and even national/societal, for example the attempt in the United Kingdom in recent years to professionalize management through the introduction of national standards and associated qualifications for managers (Silver, 1991). Finally, there appear to be few restrictions on what constitutes, conceptually and methodologically, a management development 'intervention'. To the examples already given could be added coaching, mentoring, working in action learning groups, project assignments, job shadowing, job enlargement and job rotation, to name but a few.

Beyond this, management development must be concerned not only with interventions themselves, but the processes of discernment and decision making which lead to those interventions. Therefore it is concerned with assessment, performance appraisal and other methods used to judge how an individual, team, unit or entire organization could be developed to help meet implicit or explicit managerial performance criteria. It is arguable – and this book will strongly argue – that to attempt to undertake development activity without definition of, and attention to, such criteria is at best a lottery, and at worst a reckless squandering of investment resources. Those involved with management development know that the one thing the field does not lack is offerings – from literally thousands of sources of supply – of the ways and means by which management might be developed.

Underlying assumptions

The title of the book implies that management development, despite its breadth, contradictions and complexities, *is* manageable. I shall proceed on that basis, and in so doing make four main assumptions:

1 It is both desirable and possible to generalize the principles and practices of effective management development to many, if not most, organizational contexts. Put another way, managerial work is notable more for its commonalities than its differences.

2 It is assumed that organizations which take a systematic approach to management development are more likely to move towards the achievement of an integrated Human Resource Strategy (HRS) than those that take a piecemeal approach. Although the notion of an integrated HRS may resemble an 'impossible dream' (Mabey and Salaman, 1995: 449), the surest way of achieving lack of integration – which amounts to *dis*integration – is to adopt an approach which takes no account of

the principles of good research design. That is, the approach taken will be poor if it does not pose questions or hypotheses about what might, or might not, be effective, and if it does not collect or analyse data to answer its questions or test its hypotheses. And if it does none of these things, it cannot evaluate outcomes. Regrettably, much of the real world of management development is something like Homer's *Odyssey* or Virgil's *Aeneid*: an over-long journey full of interesting but often useless and dangerous diversions, and one which many of the voyagers fail to complete.

3 There exists a substantial number of individuals who would rather make the management development journey without too many useless and dangerous diversions, while still finding it interesting, even stimulating. Foremost among these are the people in organizations who bear the responsibilities for developing others. These people are numerous, but our assertion is that the most significant person in any decision about an individual's development was always, is now, and ever shall be that individual's immediate manager. This book should therefore be of interest to general managers at all levels. It is also intended for human resources practitioners – generalists, management development specialists and consultants – and those engaged in business and organizational studies.

4 Finally, management development is something that really matters in organizations, and is therefore worthy of serious management attention. There is some fairly compelling evidence that this should be so. As will be seen in Chapter 2, organizations spend a very large amount of money trying to develop their managers. Management development is also an international phenomenon. This book is informed mainly by experience in the United Kingdom and United States, but management development practices elsewhere are receiving increased attention (Storey *et al.*, 1997; Mabey *et al.*, 1998). Undoubtedly methods and priorities vary between different national cultures and industrial environments, but the fact remains that the people who run organizations generally believe – or behave as though they believe – that what managers do is crucially important to success. They also appear to believe that the way managers operate can be improved by intervening in their lives from time to

time with offers for them to learn something new – about business, about techniques, about themselves – which will help them to perform their current or future roles more effectively. As we shall see, the idea of management development is not new, but the context in which it occurs has changed over time. At present, there is an increasing tendency towards conceptualizing one's employees as 'human capital' or 'human assets'. The terminology is borrowed from accountancy, and conveys the sense that employees represent a form of investment on which organizations should aim to maximize their return; 'labour' has become 'capital'. So if the problem now is seen to be how to make people a viable form of investment, the question is how one does it. A common response is to turn to individual development, and attempt to direct the individual towards acquiring knowledge and skills appropriate to his or her job, or a future job. A related response is to expect, and even require, that individual to share knowledge with other employees. These responses are reflected in popular expressions such as 'the learning organization' and 'knowledge management', and operationalized through the creation of new institutions called 'corporate universities' and the development of knowledge-sharing systems such as corporate Intranet sites. These devices are not, of course, aimed solely at *management* development, but the climate being created by these events is one where management development is, by definition, receiving more management attention, and probably more than in its history to date.

Organization of this book

The contents of this book are organized around three main themes. The first of these is concerned with the *context* of management development. Chapter 2 takes an historical perspective, and follows the rise of management development as it has followed the rise of management. Chapter 3 examines some definitional issues in management development, and draws attention to the problems of trying to accommodate potentially contradictory approaches within a single organization, arguing the need for a distinctive development *agenda*.

The second theme is *methodology*, and is covered by Chapters 4 to 8. The methods advocated here follow the guiding framework of McGehee and Thayer (1961), which proposes a three-level analysis of needs – organizational, job and person – to identify what development activities might be effective. Here, that framework is addressed specifically to managerial functions and roles, and consideration given to how to integrate the data obtained from needs analysis in a way which points to selection of appropriate development interventions. I give a fair amount of attention to the notion of *competency* and how competencies can be used in the assessment and development of managers. No prior knowledge of competency is assumed, but for those (perhaps few) readers who are not familiar with the thinking behind competency I strongly recommend *Designing and Achieving Competency* (Boam and Sparrow, 1992) as a highly readable introduction. Two further aspects of intervention selection are then explored: pedagogical considerations, with particular reference to learning theories and empirical support for them, and evaluation. For evaluation, a method is offered which would be taken for granted by social science researchers, but which may seem radical to many practitioners, namely that any management development intervention should be treated as though it were a *research design* from its very inception and beyond its immediate application.

The third theme is a *critical* one, and this is covered in Chapter 9. While most of the book is guided by functionalist organization theory (Burrell and Morgan, 1979), some alternative perspectives on management development are considered. Finally, and with the reminder that this book is about *managing* management development rather than just observing it, some critical questions are posed on the approach which is most likely to move organizations towards a greater degree of alignment between their desired strategic ends and their management development means. The aim of this book, therefore, is to move the reader somewhat closer towards the impossible dream of integration, but substantially further away from the nightmare of futile activity.

2

MANAGEMENT DEVELOPMENT: LONG HISTORY, SHORT CHANGE?

In comparison with such efforts (in the United States and Soviet Union), British methods of selecting, educating and training its managers seem designed to achieve a precisely opposite effect, that is to say, to produce a class composed of amateurs instead of professionals, and they seem to succeed very well in doing so.

(Rees, 1994: 43, originally published in 1963)

Recent studies of management education and training (Constable and McCormick, 1987; Handy, 1987; Osbaldeston Working Party, 1987) report a strange paradox. The value of management skills is increasingly accepted ... Yet there is apparently still very little formal effort to develop management skills.

(Salaman, 1995: 29)

The two quotations above, although over thirty years apart, appear to point to a similar problem; in Britain, the attention and effort given to developing managers has been considerably less than that given in other countries, or to other professional occupations. Indeed, in Britain management has historically not quite obtained the full standing of a 'profession', according to Reed and Anthony (1992: 592). These writers go on to say (p. 593) that:

The managerial 'class', such as it was, had become deeply embedded in a centuries-old technique and culture of rule which emphasised stability at the expense of innovation, and compromise at the expense of confrontation . . . Not only this, but British managers seemed to lack the entrepreneurial zeal and thrust, *as well as the basic technical competence,* of managerial elites elsewhere (emphasis added).

Has management development, then, failed its intended 'beneficiaries'? Before attempting to answer this question, it is worth some further exploration of the occupational group which is the object of development. What are 'managers' and what types of knowledge, skills and abilities do they need to demonstrate in order to be considered 'developed'?

The elusive phenomenon of management

The division of labour and power between those who 'do' and those who 'control' has, as Russell (1940: 16) long ago asserted: '. . . always existed in human communities, as far back as our knowledge extends . . . Most collective enterprises are only possible if they are directed by some governing body'. However, what made management become a familiar, common occupational description was the confluence in the nineteenth century of the advance in natural sciences and the 'growth of a vigorous capitalistic economy which employed the discoveries of science for private profit' (Miller and Form, 1950: 114). A third factor, perhaps an outcome of the first two, was the invention of the public limited liability company, which allowed the separation of the owners of capital – the shareholders – from those responsible for earning a return on it through the management of resources. Chandler (1990: 96) observed that as recently as 1840 there were almost no salaried managers, the control of enterprises being exercised by owners, either as partners or major shareholders in their organizations. Within 20 to 30 years, however, companies had begun to shift strongly towards the modern enterprise model, employing 'a hierarchy of middle and top-salaried managers who supervise the work under its control and who form an entire new class of businessman' (1990: 96) and who 'planned and carried out the strategy of growth, which, in turn, increased the number of executives at all managerial levels within the enterprise' (1990: 115).

Today the title of 'manager' is applied to millions of jobs in all types of organization, whether publicly or privately owned. 'Management' covers a wide range of job titles, as deemed appropriate to rank and function: 'supervisor', 'section head', 'team leader' 'finance director' and so on. Indeed, in some organizations, 'management' is synonymous with the attainment of a particular *level*, whether the function performed involves controlling staff or not (Hales, 1986: 89). Management is commonly construed as the basis for a career (Nicholson and West, 1988; Gowler and Legge, 1991) and has been described by Mitroff (1998: 68) as 'the most important of all human activities'.

Why then, when management appears to be a universally well established and common occupation, and a distinct career form, could it possibly be conceived as 'elusive'? The problem, it seems, is that there remains some difficulty in identifying what it is that managers actually *do*. In a seminal treatment of this subject, Hales (1986) rigorously examined the extant research evidence and concluded that:

> The ... weakness of existing studies is that it is uncertain whether they identify exclusively *managerial* behaviour. No study has sought to compare managers and non-managers and, thereby identify the *differentia specifica* of their work. Moreover, because of the absence of consistent categories or models, *post hoc* comparisons between studies of individual occupations cannot be made. The possibility that the work described in studies of managers is not definitely 'managerial' is both generally unfortunate and specifically so in that the evidence cannot be used to address the issue ... of whether 'management' is an inextricable element of all kinds of work, and hence part of any occupation, or whether it is a distinct and separable activity, amenable to allocations to one particular category of worker. In short, the studies have not demonstrated that there is a bounded and separable set of activities which may be called 'managerial work' – and not merely activities which managers have been shown to do.
>
> (Hales, 1986: 109)

Now if Hales's conclusions are sound, then those of us involved in management development have a problem. If we cannot accurately discriminate between managerial and other types of work, how can we develop people to be more effective managers? This is a problem with which those who attempt to practise management development are all too familiar. In my experience, many programmes which are offered as 'management development' for employees of upper middle and senior rank could be more accurately (but more clumsily) entitled 'programmes from which we hope that most senior people, regardless of function, will learn something useful'. There is a danger that what is offered at such courses is not so much grounded in real job requirements as in a socially constructed 'executive world'. Here, the participants are released from their real work for four or five days to indulge in games, introspection (often abetted by the use of psychological 'tests' of dubious theoretical pedigree), corporate socialization, hospitality and exposure to a sample of current fashion in management 'thinking', as espoused by some of the better-known gurus. The best that the organizers of such events can hope for – and, indeed, which they *do* earnestly hope for – is that the participants go away 'happy' (Mole, 1996: 21).

The supply side of management development

The apparent difficulty in trying to define with any precision what managers do does not inhibit the creators and suppliers of management development 'solutions', it seems. Indeed, it could be argued that the researcher's difficulties – 'the plethora of categories for describing the phenomenon, the difficulty of judging the appropriateness of the behaviour identified and, finally, the problem of whether the work described is exclusively "managerial" ' (Hales, 1986: 111) – are heaven-sent opportunities for the inventors of training and development methods. An idea which will be examined in the next chapter, that management action is 'driven by plausibility rather than accuracy' (Weick, 1995: 55), could help to explain why so many methods for developing managers have been introduced and tried over the years.

Huczynski (1983) lists and describes over *400* management

development methods. And every passing management fashion (Gill and Whittle, 1993: 287) such as total quality management or core process redesign brings, in the wake of its founding gurus, cohorts of 'consultants' offering solutions (Sturdy, 1995: 1). This will often include highly stylized, prescriptive training for management in how to implement these solutions, often in conjunction with the formation of implementation 'project teams' or 'task forces'. Given this ability of management and management development to feed off one another, it is not surprising that management development has become a high-revenue undertaking, and that over 90 per cent of organizations engage in some form of management development activity (Tannenbaum and Yukl, 1992; Baldwin and Padgett, 1994).

These writers were referring to their observation of the United States rather than the United Kingdom, but there is evidence that the management development business in the UK, though fragmented, is well developed. The *Management Training Directory* (1997), which lists management training providers and their offerings, gives details of over 1100 different suppliers which claim to offer management training in some shape or form. These include institutional providers, such as the business schools of universities and colleges of further education, professional bodies such as the Institute of Management, large and medium-sized training firms and smaller 'consultancies'. The vast majority of these providers employ fewer than 10 people. It is worth noting that the directory does not claim to be comprehensive, so the suppliers listed represent a sample (but probably a large one) of the total number in the UK.

The directory also lists the 'public courses' offered by these suppliers. Although it becomes clear from an examination of this list that not all these courses are strictly concerned with managerial knowledge, skills and abilities (for example, they include computing and sales skills), nevertheless over 3600 courses are on offer which have a primary managerial focus (e.g., 'general management', 'project management', 'leadership and team building' and industry-specific management training). The vast majority are very short courses – between one and five days – designed around a single main subject. The list also includes longer vocational programmes, such as a Certificate or Diploma in Management, offered by public colleges of further or higher education. Recall, again, that 3600 is not the total number of management courses publicly offered in the UK; it is only those listed in the directory.

Most of the programmes offered as public courses are also made available 'in-company', i.e., delivered to a particular organization's employees, and usually with the suggestion that they will be tailored to that organization's particular needs. For the record, the directory also lists 91 sources of MBA programmes, 142 suppliers of materials (such as audio-visual equipment, training videos and books) and 192 venue providers, many of which offer multiple locations for holding courses. From the size of these data, the amount of management training activity in the UK each year is considerable, and merits the term 'industry', albeit a highly heterogeneous one. In the absence of any hard financial data, if we were to estimate conservatively that the average revenue for each of the 1100 providers were £200,000 per year, then their total annual revenues would amount to £220m. Adding estimated revenues from MBAs, sales of materials and hire of venues, we should expect total annual revenues for the sample of suppliers in the directory to be in the order of £500m at least. Now, bearing in mind that this is a sample of the supply side, and does not include the amount that companies spend on their *internal* management development resources, nor their facilities and other overheads, nor the opportunity costs of days spent in training by managers, then I do not consider it beyond belief that the money spent on management training and education in the UK exceeds £1 billion every year.

To check the veracity of that figure, we can work it back through a different reasoning process. An Institute of Management Research Board report (1995) estimated that the size of the UK managerial labour pool was between 2 and 2.25 million. Taking the higher figure as the denominator, and our £1 billion expenditure estimate as the numerator, this would mean that the average amount of money spent on management training and education per UK manager per year is just under £450. This seems low, especially as a survey of 2051 UK managers by Warr (1994: 1) showed that the median number of days' training received by each manager was eight. However, the sample was made up of members of the Institute of Management, individuals who probably consider themselves professional managers and who could be expected to make efforts to ensure that they receive training each year. Indeed, 88 per cent of the sample undertook some training in 1992. Compare this with a different study, also cited by Warr (Employment Department, 1990: 55), that only 48 per cent of UK managers and professional workers received training in a three-year period. This is corroborated by a finding in the Institute of Management Research Board report (1995: 25) that 'over half of all UK companies appear to make no formal provision for the training of their managers'. If the £1 billion+ of training expense is being spent on only half the UK's managers, then the cost per manager trained approaches £1000, which begins to look more realistic.

Clearly, the above estimates are highly speculative, and perhaps it would be wise not to use them to make comparisons with, say, other countries' expenditure on management training and development. But since comparisons are always interesting (and the more invidious, the more interesting), a 1992 survey of 66 US Fortune 500 companies (Vicere *et al.*, 1994: 8) found that the median annual expense per individual enrolled in an in-company programme was $5000 (about £3150) and per individual enrolled in a university-based programme it was $20,000 (about £12,600). Eighty-seven per cent of the responding companies offered 'in-company executive education activities' (1994: 9).

Returning to Salaman's (1995) paradox cited at the start of this chapter, we can now add another intriguing ingredient: the value of management skills is increasingly accepted but there is very uneven *formal* effort to develop them, despite a considerable amount of activity generated, and money earned, by the UK management training industry. How can this be? Our earlier analysis about the nature of the problem can be used to generate some possible reasons:

1 In spite of its success and ubiquity, managerial work has (and just possibly its practitioners have) so far defied meaningful definition as to its nature and content.
2 The consequences of a loosely defined construct of management are loosely defined constructs of management performance, job requirement criteria and development needs.

3 Organizations recognize the salience of management as a significant variable in their performance, but given the definition
difficulties in 1 and 2 above, tend to select ready-made, short-
duration 'solutions' off the training industry's 'shelf' as their
means of developing managers.

4 Such 'counterfactual thinking' is not unusual, indeed it is quite
normal (Branscombe *et al.*, 1997). The problem here is one of
management *uncertainty*. As we shall see in the following chapter, helping an organization to cope with uncertainty is a source
of organizational value and power. Because the nature of managerial work is uncertain, it follows that there is a real opportunity for those who are prepared to render it less uncertain to
bring perceived value to the organization, and greater organizational influence to themselves. Herein, then, lies the essence of
successful management development activity: to be able to
comprehend and articulate what managers *should do, in the
context of one's particular organization*. The quest for this will be
pursued throughout this book. Meanwhile, a brief historical
summary of how various writers have prescribed managerial
work – and developers have responded – will serve as an introduction to this topic.

The management function prescribed

As we move into the twenty-first century it could be seen as
impressive (and for others, perhaps, as depressing) that the writers on management from the earlier part of the twentieth century
(e.g. Taylor, 1947; Fayol, 1949; Urwick, 1952) still influence so
strongly the way people – including managers – think about
management. These writers, who were active and influential from
the time of the Great War, tended to analyse what functions managers should discharge rather than the specific activities needed to
perform them. Nor did they state what individuals should bring
to those activities to perform them successfully. The management
functions, according to Fayol, could be categorized into what
Carroll and Gillen (1987: 38) call the five 'classical management
functions': planning, organizing, commanding, coordinating and
controlling. The language of management functions here looks

strangely militaristic. If, instead of classical *management* functions, one substituted *military leadership*, the descriptions of the functions would still fit very well. However, this is no coincidence. The military world provides an enduring model of organization for management, as testified by the way that military terminology – words like 'strategy', 'logistics', 'targets', 'objectives', 'capability', 'arena', 'escalation' – provides management with some of its most cherished clichés. Weber (1990: 9–10), writing in 1924, noted that 'the modern army is essentially a bureaucratic organization administered by that peculiar type of military functionary, the "officer"'. Consider also Pugh's (1990: 179) observation:

> Fayol . . . was the first of modern management writers to propound a theoretical analysis of what managers have to do and by what principles they have to do it; an analysis which has withstood half a century of critical discussion. His principles of *authority and responsibility, unity of command, good order, esprit de corps,* etc. are the common currency of management parlance (emphasis added).

Carroll and Gillen (1987) agree with Pugh about Fayol's staying power, noting that the vast majority of contemporary American management textbooks utilize his classification to organize their text and to examine the nature of managerial work. They state that 'the classical functions still represent the most useful way of conceptualising the manager's job, *especially for management education*' (p. 48) (emphasis added).

Reading Fayol's work today, it is not difficult to see the reason for its enduring attraction. He presents his prescriptions in a matter-of-fact, common-sense style. Take the following example on planning:

> Thinking out a plan and ensuring its success is one of the keenest satisfactions for an intelligent man to experience . . . This power of thinking out and executing is what is called initiative, and freedom to propose and to execute belongs, too, each in its way, to initiative . . .
>
> Much tact and some integrity are required to inspire everyone's initiative, within the limits imposed by respect for authority and for discipline.
>
> (1990: 199)

Fayol was clearly writing for, and addressing himself to, *managers* (as opposed to, say, academics). F. W. Taylor did likewise, and the tradition of highly prescriptive management writing continues to this day, sometimes with conspicuous success, as in the *In Search of Excellence* phenomenon (see Guest, 1992: 5–19). This rhetorical (as opposed to theory-based) approach is likely to get management heads nodding; it sounds and feels 'right'. For management developers, however, it presents a major problem because it is extremely difficult to operationalize lofty rhetoric into statements or definitions of desired *behaviour* by managers. Taking the extract from Fayol quoted above, what does 'thinking out a plan' actually involve? What does 'successful' planning look like? How would we recognize 'much tact' and 'some integrity' – and how would we *model* these abilities to management trainees? As Mintzberg (1990: 223) comments on Fayol's classification of functions, they 'tell us little about what managers actually do. At best they indicate some vague objectives managers have when they work.'

There is a second, equally difficult, problem with the classical school of prescriptive writers, again with consequences for management development. They tend to convey the idea, attributed to F. W. Taylor, of 'the one best way' – that any and all managerial problems can be reduced, and optimally 'solved', through application of the most appropriate method. It is ironic that such thinking should have been termed – and continues to be termed – 'scientific management'. For, although Taylor's approach was nothing if not rigorously empirical in its pursuit of the one best way, it took nothing from, and contributed nothing to, any testable theories of behaviour at work, managerial or otherwise. Taylor was fonder of 'principles' than hypotheses (Taylor, 1990: 203–22), and by his own admission not too concerned that the academic community did not take kindly to his use of the word 'science' to classify his principles. In effect, what Taylor posited was that in any task, the most significant variable in terms of outcome was method; if the method were 'right' – and the right method, the one best way, could always be found by experiment – then the outcome would be optimal. The possibility that the outcome might be contingent on other variables, over which the individual manager might have little or no control, was not considered.

As early as 1929, the one best way argument was incurring criticism both on scientific and ethical grounds (Myers, 1956: 102–7). Since then, the idea that outcomes are contingent on other salient variables has been widely researched, from a number of perspectives, including technological complexity (Woodward, 1958), structure (Burns and Stalker, 1961), industry/sector environment (Lawrence and Lorsch, 1986) and national culture (Hofstede, 1990). There now exists a substantial amount of research evidence that, at the very least, the factors which contribute to an organizational outcome being judged a success (given that the meaning of 'success' is, itself, open to wider interpretation) are more numerous and complex than the prescriptive writers either knew about, or chose to admit. Yet the school of prescriptive writing goes on, to this day. The shelves of airport bookstalls groan with anecdotal tracts, often telling the stories of management 'heroes', and purporting to offer managers insight into organizational and personal success. Programmatic approaches to the handling of organizational change – total quality management, core process redesign – rise and fall, like the hemlines of fashion.

This is not the place to explore this disturbing phenomenon (see Watson, 1994 for an incisive review), but the message for management developers should be clear: beware of prescriptive writers and the gifts they bring. Their edicts are difficult to turn into meaningful criteria and methods by which to develop managers, and they tend towards over-simplification, ignoring or understating variables which could have effects on managerial and organizational performance. I take the view that the richest source of meaningful data about the performance and development needs of managers is to research them in the specific context in which they actually perform, that is in the organization for which they work, and its environment.

Having warned of the dangers of prescription, it is only fair to warn that this book will now take a slightly more prescriptive turn. It will state the need for practitioners to establish a clear and distinctive management development agenda for their organizations. It will go on to propose a methodology for identifying management development needs, looking first at the needs and environment of the employing organization. It will then discuss techniques for accessing development needs for management roles performed in the organization with particular reference to the use of competency modelling as a method of high-level job analysis for managerial roles. (Note, however, that the use of this methodology is not restricted to managerial roles, and can be equally well applied to others.) Finally, it will evaluate some methods for accessing the development needs of *individuals* who perform, or are about to perform, a management role. Our emphasis will be on *behaviour*, and how to describe and distinguish more effective from less effective management behaviours, but always within the context of the employing organization. I do not advocate, like some of the writers mentioned earlier, any universalistic 'rights' and 'wrongs'. Before leaving the field of concepts of management there is, however, one other monster walking abroad which causes great difficulties for management developers and, if it cannot be slain, it should at least be challenged.

The 'management' versus 'leadership' argument

This argument may have been around for a long time, but it was a Harvard Business Review article – 'Managers and leaders: are they different?' – (Zaleznik, 1992) which brought it into focus. Although, as for most literature, the author's messages – or individual constructions put upon them – have probably been quoted far more often than the article has actually been read, the messages are, in this author's experience, influential. They are recited in expressions such as 'I consider myself to be a leader rather than a manager', or 'I much prefer leadership to management.' Zaleznik has successfully created or reinforced a dichotomy with the rhetorical question he puts into the title of his article. And the response of many, when presented with this putative dichotomy, is to opt for 'leadership', and consign the role of management from the bridge of the vessel to its engine room. Zaleznik's arguments therefore bear some examination.

One which recurs throughout the piece is that a managerial 'culture' tends to emphasize rationality and control at the expense of individualism. He characterizes two distinct 'personalities': 'It takes neither genius nor heroism to be a manager but rather persistence, tough-mindedness, hard work, intelligence, analytical ability, and perhaps most important, tolerance and goodwill' (1992: 127). Leaders are far more mysterious, complex creatures: '... leadership is a psychodrama in which a brilliant, lonely person must gain control of himself or herself as a precondition for controlling others' (p. 127). Zaleznik does not reach out to any specific theories of personality to support his assertions (to be fair, he was writing for managers), but his conclusion is that: 'There are no known ways to "train" great leaders' (p. 127). Perhaps, therefore, management developers should give up at this point or limit their ambition to making that lesser breed of managers more persistent, tough-minded and hard working. Or perhaps they should concentrate on management selection, using every tool which psychodynamic or trait theories of personality can furnish to predict 'leadership' behaviour. And leaders do behave differently to managers, according to Zaleznik:

> Where managers act to limit choices, leaders develop from approaches to long-standing problems and open issues to new options. To be effective, leaders must project their ideas onto images that excite people and only then develop choices that give those images substance.

As might be expected, Zaleznik concludes that 'leaders' have a different effect on others than do 'managers':

> Consequently, one often hears subordinates characterise managers as inscrutable, detached and manipulative. These adjectives arise from the subordinates' perception that they are united together in a process whose purpose is to maintain a controlled as well as rational and equitable structure.
> In contrast, one often hears leaders referred to with adjectives rich in emotional content. Leaders attract strong feelings of intensity or of love and hate. Human relations in leader-dominated structures often appear turbulent, intense, and at times even disorganized. Such an atmosphere intensifies individual motivation and often produces unexpected outcomes.
> (Zaleznik, 1992: 132)

Although Zaleznik avoids using the word, the effect he is describing here is usually termed 'charismatic', and herein lies a problem. As Smith and Peterson put it:

The principal difficulty in evaluating the success of current attempts to revive the concept of charismatic leadership remains one of definition. It has been well established . . . that *subordinates respond to leaders with whom they can establish warm and friendly relations* . . . the relationship of supervisor consideration to performance measures is much more varied. What is not clear is whether researchers into charisma have succeeded in identifying a style of leadership which is different from supervisor warmth.

(Smith and Peterson, 1988: 117, emphasis added)

Like others who favour the polemic of the 'one best way', Zaleznik illustrates his arguments with 'great men' anecdotes, and generalizations, rather than references to specific theories or empirical studies. From his conclusion on how leadership is developed, we are really only left with two possibilities: that the individual, at some stage in his or her life, should form a 'deep attachment to a great teacher or other person who understands and has the ability to communicate with the gifted individual' (p. 133), or benefit from mentoring by a senior executive (p. 134), which may well amount to the same thing. Now, nobody should deny the importance of leadership, however defined (and Smith and Peterson (1988) provide a thorough analysis), to organizational performance. But to suggest that management and leadership are fundamentally separate sets of behaviours, grounded in deep individual differences and tied into totally separate roles, is asking for trouble, particularly when the statement 'I think I am more of a leader than a manager' is later discovered to mean 'I do not wish to be in a position where I have to hold anyone accountable for performance.' The ability to lead is not confined to managerial roles, but my contention is that it is integral to every managerial role, even though notions of effective leadership will differ according to organization, national culture, or even the situation in which the manager finds him/herself (Fiedler, 1990).

Nor should we claim that certain aspects of leadership popularly attributed to 'charisma' are without value. The ability to sketch a compelling vision of the future and articulate it in a way which motivates others to act is not without its uses. But it is not enough, and needs to be complemented by the ability to implement actions over the long haul. Those who manage management development should acknowledge – and perhaps take comfort from – the fact that their role is to nurture and develop a range of knowledge, skills and abilities in their management population, of which leadership is a crucial part, but a *part*. They should also take care to read critically any offerings which come their way headed 'leadership training' or 'leadership development', looking particularly at what outcomes are promised or implied, and even more particularly if there is a suggestion that the participants will emerge from the intervention behaving more like the Zaleznik 'leader' figure.

3

THE MANAGEMENT DEVELOPMENT AGENDA

Training, education and development distinguished

Given the definitional problems noted in the Introduction, it is unlikely that the subject of management development will be free from controversies, and indeed it is not. Before looking at some of these, it would be as well to attempt some meaningful definition of the term *management development* which distinguishes it from two other terms which are often used interchangeably with it: *management training* and *management education*. A useful distinction between the terms training, education and development is made by Phillips (1987: 149–51), drawing on earlier work by Nadler (1980). This model differentiates each of the three terms according to three categories: *focus* (job or organizational requirement addressed), *economic classification* (type of expenditure) and *risk level*. Using this classification, the focus of *training* is the employee's present job, where the aim is to raise performance to the standard required by the job's performance criteria, for example as set out in a job description. It is deemed to have a quick payback (if successful) and is therefore classed as a short-term expense item, and represents a low risk. In management terms 'training', thus construed, lies very much in the territory of short off-the-job courses, such as how to conduct employee appraisals to a corporate standard.

The focus of *education* is the employee's *future* job, with the intention of providing learning experiences which prepare the employee for transition to a specific, usually higher level, role. Here, the economic classification is one of 'short-term investment', which carries a medium level of risk. Phillips does not put a timescale on 'short-term', but in accounting it is conventionally a period up to 12 months, and this gives a fair indication. In management terms, examples of 'education' in the United Kingdom are the programmes provided by institutions of further and higher education leading to formal management qualifications such as the Certificate or Diploma in Management (aligned to Management Charter Initiative standards) or the Diploma in Management Studies (DMS). Such programmes address areas of knowledge (finance, people, information, operations) and skill (personal effectiveness) with the purpose of qualifying trainees for demanding managerial roles in their organizations (see Salaman, 1995: 43). Depending on the learning method used, these qualifications take about 12 to 18 months to complete.

Whereas for training and education Phillips takes *job* as the unit of analysis, for development he takes *organization*. As he puts it:

> Development focuses on the organization and future organizational activities. It is based on the assumption that organizations must grow and change in order to remain viable. Development programmes prepare individuals to move in the new directions that organizational change may require. They are investments for which it is almost impossible to calculate a return; and because of this, they are high-risk ventures. Developmental activities are long-range in scope and are provided without reference to a particular job. True developmental experiences are not common in most organizations, at least on any formal basis.
>
> (Phillips, 1987: 150)

Storey *et al.* (1997: 22), from a comparative study of management development practices in British and Japanese companies, remarked that 'training is not the same as development'. Whereas

British companies tended to offer training courses to their managers,

> ... what tended to be lacking was where a course might lead
> and how it would fit in with a manager's career development.
> The Japanese firms had integrated the idea of development
> into the whole way in which they operated ...

Given the apparently tenuous nature and rarity of Phillips's 'development activities' in western organizations, would we fare better by giving attention to the more tangible and shorter term objectives of training and education? My response is no, on three counts. First, I contend that development – and management development in particular – is never an end in itself, but one of many means available which might enable organizations to meet whatever performance criteria they seek to attain – survival, growth, increased profitability or productivity, and so on. Therefore it is appropriate that the *organization* should be the primary object of development. Indeed, it has been argued forcibly (see, for example, Katz and Kahn, 1978: 658; Bramley, 1992: 5) that trying to change organizations by changing individuals is conceptually flawed and practically ineffective.

Second, a long-term future focus is entirely appropriate for management development, which can be likened to, or considered as, one element of Organization Development (OD): 'a long-range, planned, and substantial effort that unfolds according to strategy' (French *et al.*, 1989: 9). If this approach is taken, then management development may be conceived as a potent instrument of organizational change, rather than a set of interesting and entertaining activities arranged for managers by the training department, which in my experience it frequently is (Mole, 1996).

Finally, expenditure on management development should be considered as a long-term *investment* rather than as an accumulation of short-term expense items. This notion may have considerable intuitive appeal to those who manage management development, not least because the seasoned practitioners among them will frequently have seen development picked out as a soft target of cost reduction campaigns, and they may well concur with Rainbird's (1994: 87) observation that 'the financial procedures introduced to account for training expenditure may make this kind of investment vulnerable to cost-cutting'. However, if management developers are willing to embrace and live by this investment arrangement, they must equally be prepared to die by it. To claim that one's activities represent an 'investment' to the organization requires that those activities should be subject to the strictures of investment evaluation. As Weston and Brigham (1982: 284) put it:

> In most firms there are more proposals for projects than the firm is able or willing to finance. Some proposals are good, others are poor, and methods must be developed for distinguishing between the good and the poor. Essentially, the end product is a ranking of the proposals and the cut-off point for determining how far down the ranked list to go . . . Thus, an estimate of benefits is required, and a method for converting the benefits into a ranking measure must be developed.

This theme will be examined again later when I come to consider how to evaluate the utility of management development (Chapter 8). For the moment, the point is emphasized that, among the range of ways available for organizations to invest money to develop themselves, management development is but one option, and it is in competition with others to prove its particular benefits. It may, as I suggested earlier, be currently coming (back) into vogue thanks to the diffusion of 'learning organization' rhetoric, but management fashions are notoriously transient (Gill and Whittle, 1993) and the wise practitioner should not rely on lightweight thinking for protection when the economic climate for training and development starts turning rough again, as it inevitably will.

Practitioners might well agree with, and publicly espouse, the bringing of the three dimensions of organizational, longitudinal and investment focus together to underpin management development. But they might go on privately believing in a rather different 'theory-in-use, which is the one they actually use when they act' (Argyris, 1990: 23), which emphasizes 'pragmatism', 'common sense' or 'realism', particularly if they can sense a threat to the survival of the management development function and measure their success solely in terms of creating 'feel-good' reactions among the managers who attend their training programmes.

Argyris argues that when such theories-in-use are non-evaluative and make no attempt to link cause and effect explicitly – for example, 'that's just the way it is round here' – then this will routinely lead to defensive behaviour among organizational members. I would argue that, in the world of management development, it will lead to *accommodating* behaviour by practitioners; that when a suggestion for a new training course is made by a senior executive (or by a training supplier who has the ear of senior executives) the management developer often attempts to accommodate the suggestion because to do so is deemed to be politically realistic. The result of too much accommodation will be a mish-mash of short-term programmes and numerous sources of supply, where the main concern is how to administer it all effectively rather than how to meet the development needs of managers.

How can such a state of affairs be avoided, or overcome? This is perhaps the toughest of all problems for those who manage management development, and goes far beyond conventional wisdom and the usual managerialist ideology, into the nature of power and influence in organizations. This issue will be considered in greater depth later, but one particularly useful source is the concept of 'sensemaking' (Weick, 1993; 1995). The management developer needs to convince the dominant coalition in the organization that the views and actions s/he asks them to endorse are, within that organization's context, *plausible*:

> Even if accuracy were important, executives seldom produce it. From the point of view of sensemaking, that is no big problem. The strength of sensemaking as a perspective derives from the fact that it does not rely on accuracy and its model is not object perception. Instead, sensemaking is about plausibility, pragmatics, coherence, reasonableness, creation, invention and instrumentality
>
> (Weick, 1995: 57)

This may mean demonstrating that management development plans and activities are consistent with the organization's goals and values as expressed in a mission statement or business plan. It may mean explaining a recent organizational crisis (for example an unexpected and dramatic downturn in profits leading to the elimination of senior individuals) in terms of a deficiency in the management development process (for example insufficient attention to succession planning) and using that as a lever to initiate a new approach. It may also mean using plausibility to deny access to the management development agenda of the pet interventions of others. My experience is that it is difficult to resist the suggestions of very senior executives about management development programmes and processes. They are often made as generalizations based on very small samples, such as 'I myself learned a lot from this course, and everyone else will.' For the management developer to counter such a suggestion with the argument that, based on rigorous analysis of organizational needs, it does not fit in with the human resources grand plan might be a courageous stand for principle and objectivity, but also a career-limiting mistake. It is also just feasible that the senior executive's proposal 'makes sense'. As Weick observes '. . . some kinds of sense may contradict other kinds. That is not surprising given the independence of diverse projects and the fact that their pursuit in tandem can work at cross-purposes' (1995: 27).

The management developer must therefore acknowledge, and respond to, the need of sensemakers such as senior managers for 'values, priority and clarity about preferences to help them be clear about *which projects matter*' (Weick, 1995: 27–8, emphasis added). Unless s/he is able to clarify for the power system that a specific proposal is at odds with stated direction or organizational values (e.g., 'this programme will not help us in the pursuit of the intellectual leadership we aspire to in our mission statement'), or with priorities ('this could divert us from our commitment to existing agreed plans'), then the 'sense' of the new proposal could prevail. The management developer must have a distinctive agenda.

The management development agenda

Kotter (1982), from his study of senior general managers, observed that the successful ones had developed distinctive agendas about what they wanted to accomplish. In the same way, the management developer needs an agenda which can stand up to most of the vicissitudes of senior executive sensemaking. The nature of that agenda will be contingent on organizational factors – values, strategies, priorities and preferences – but I argue here that, unless it is thoughtfully constructed, well-articulated and robust, the developer's agenda will surely be side-tracked by the agendas of others. As Lukes (1986: 9) puts it:

> . . . one exercises power . . . by controlling the agenda, mobilising the bias of the system, determining which issues are 'key' issues, indeed which issues come up for decision, and excluding those which threaten the interests of the powerful.

What organizational contingencies *are* important, and how the management developer recognizes and works with them, are highly situational and therefore beyond prescription (though not beyond guidance as to their diagnosis – see Chapter 4). However, I advocate that by adopting certain tenets the developer is more likely to establish a credible agenda. I suggest four:

First, management development, like organization development, should be represented as *a long-term process*. I agree with Campbell *et al.* (1970: 4) that 'management is the key occupational group in an industrial society', and that it is still the case in most organizations, as it was nearly 30 years ago, that 'presently, the supply of managerial talent falls short of meeting demand'. This chronic shortfall of managerial ability means that an important function of management development is to try to minimize its adverse impact on the organization over time.

Second, because management development is concerned with the *supply* of managerial talent to the organization, it is a wide-ranging process which is far from synonymous with 'training'. It should be concerned, for example, with the *intake* of managers, or potential managers, into the organization at the point of recruitment. It should be concerned with the *assessment* of managers to identify their development needs, or to consider their suitability for promotion or assignments. Similarly, the *appraisal* of managers should provide sources of decision making about development. So far as actions taken to increase the knowledge, skills and abilities of managers are concerned, development should be an overriding concept, subsuming education and training (as previously defined), and all other interventions such as project assignments, temporary transfers, job shadowing and so on.

Third, as I asserted in the Introduction, the most influential force for developing managers in any organization is its management, not the individual or department labelled 'management development'. All the key processes for developing managers 'belong', properly, to management. I have also noted, however, that talented management is in short supply and managers, according to Mintzberg (1973: 51) feel 'compelled to perform a great quantity of work at an unrelenting pace'. They are expected to perform a great variety of activities and live 'continuously with an awareness of what else might or must be done at any time'. They therefore often need help, in the form of advice from professional management development people who, as well as acting as advisers, are usually charged with delivery of a service of some type, perhaps in the form of projects, programmes and other interventions. So it is not uncommon for the person responsible for management development to have to manage resources, including internal professionals and administrators and external resources such as consultants and contractors. Usually, too, management developers will be expected to operate within the constraints of financial budgets. The developer's credentials depend not only on the counsel given *to* the management team but, by virtue of the role performed, on membership *of* the management team, and on sharing many of the interests and values of other managers in the organization. Handling this 'inside: outside' duality is probably one of the most difficult tensions to manage successfully. Should developers veer too strongly towards the 'inside', they may tend to accommodate too readily, as noted earlier, and be seen to lack objectivity. If they tend towards the 'outside' they could be seen as over-theoretical, insufficiently pragmatic, and draw down the ultimate insult of being too 'academic'.

Fourth, within an organization, management development is part of a political system, and is more likely to be successful if it comprehends how the system works, and how to work the system – if it 'focuses attention on the environment as a source of power and on networks as both sources of power and a critical mechanism through which influence gets accomplished' (Pfeffer, 1989: 383). Without an established basis of organizational power, the developer will find that his or her agenda is too often overcome by the agendas of others. Note that the issue here is the basis of *organizational* power of the management development function, not the *personal* power of the management developer or members of the development team, though the two issues are inextricably linked. The work of Hinings *et al.* (1974) and Pfeffer (1981) on power in organizations can be used to frame some specific questions about the power and influence of management development:

Does it control resources which are seen to be of value to the organization?

The sense of this question is more political than economic, and is related to the type of work performed and the level at which management development operates. Just because work is deemed 'necessary' does not automatically make it valued. Are more time and energy spent on activities such as advising senior management on what interventions would help them achieve the business changes they seek, or booking people onto training courses? The 'taken-for-granted' activities have to be done somewhere, of course, but not necessarily by the management development function, and they must not be allowed to obstruct, prevent or discourage the higher level activities.

Does it help the organization to cope with uncertainty?

This is a particular form of value, related to the extent to which managers depend on management development to strengthen their confidence, or reduce their anxiety, in thinking about and planning for the future. This is not the type of role which has been traditionally associated with the human resources function in general, nor with management development in particular. Of the service people in organizations it has usually been the accountants to whom senior managers have looked most for shedding light on the darkness ahead (Armstrong, 1991). There is, however, some evidence that human resources people are beginning to be used more often as corporate seers, rather than merely as service providers, and this reflects some success they have had in reconstructing themselves from their erstwhile personae of 'personnel' and 'training' (Kamoche, 1994). One area of interest for the management developer is that of succession, especially of very senior people. Succession can be a major source of uncertainty and anxiety, so much so that senior management may be reluctant even to discuss it, let alone formally plan to do something about it. According to Pfeffer (1989: 391), '. . . succession, particularly at higher administrative levels, is a political event'. If one senior executive's leaving raises the possibility of having to bring in a replacement from outside the organization, there will be even greater uncertainty. Wiersema (1992: 89) concluded from her study of the relationship between the nature of executive succession and subsequent changes in organization strategy that 'introducing a new individual into the top management group provides a means for altering the nature of strategic decision-making within the organization'. And as Kesner and Dalton (1994: 704) observe, 'high levels of change in top executive positions escalate concerns over security, status and power for those remaining, and new incumbents often find it difficult to allay these fears'.

One powerful way in which the management developer can reduce this fear and uncertainty is to establish a process for developing a pool of individuals, some of whom could – all things being equal – succeed to the most senior positions, and to ensure that the existing senior incumbents manage that process effectively. Just how this might be accomplished is considered in greater depth in Chapter 4.

Is it difficult to replace?

This is the ultimate test of the value of those who carry out management development in the organization. A different, but related, question is: 'Would management development be easy to eliminate completely?' It was noted earlier how training may be vulnerable to cost cutting, and the cuts can sometimes be so deep as to terminate management development life completely. There is, too, a constant – often implicit and unspoken – threat that management development, like computer operations, catering, printing and the rest – could be readily contracted out to external providers. In the face of such a threat, it is tempting for the management developer to counter it by appeals to reason, and to a 'track record' of past achievements. If the developer does this s/he will be trying to counter rhetoric with reason, and may well be left puzzled and dismayed when rhetoric 'wins'. The legitimacy of management development may not depend on an assessment of its objective contribution so much as views of those in power of what types of activity give the organization legitimacy. Alvesson (1993: 1003) calls such views 'myths':

> These rationalised myths exercise a strong impact on formal organizations, which are obliged to respond through developing the 'right' structures, including professions, programmes and technologies. Organizations 'must' have, for example, personnel departments and functionaries, management development programmes and modern technologies, otherwise legitimacy problems arise.

The developer's task then, in rendering the management development function difficult to replace, is to ensure that attempts to question its legitimacy are not only countered, but also extinguished. How? Here, we meet another paradox. While most of this book will argue the virtues of a systematic, functionally based approach to management development, it is hard to deny Alvesson's (1993: 1013) assertion that 'in contemporary business life some of the key elements of bureaucracy as well as science and professionalism – rationality, order, predictability – seem to be less popular than virtues such as change, innovation and creativity'. The challenge for management developers, then – and for management services specialists in general – is to *perform* their role in a way which leads to objective results for their organizations, and at the same time *represent* their role as being entirely consonant with whatever management ideology is prevalent in the organization. Not only that, they must represent it as providing a unique source of value in the organization's quest for whatever goals it has set for itself. Cynical though it may seem, there is a strong vein of truth in Goffman's (1990: 29) comment that 'we know that in service occupations practitioners who may otherwise be sincere are sometimes forced to delude their customers because their customers show such a heartfelt demand for it'.

To summarize, then, I have used the notion of *agenda* to draw attention to factors which those who manage management

31

development need to keep uppermost in mind. I have argued, first, the need for a clear conceptual distinction between management development, education and training such that development – the process and investment applied to raise the effectiveness of the organization's managerial resources over time – is the dominant idea, one which guides choices and decisions about all interventions, regardless of target or duration. Management development plans and activities must be *plausible* in the current and foreseeable context of the organization. They must appear to 'make sense' and not be easily derailed by the projects of others. Moreover, management developers must themselves be plausible, maintaining credibility as to their professional ability and to their standing as members of the management team. Finally, to accomplish its goals, management development needs a relatively stable base of organizational power, attributable to the value it brings through its resources, its ability to help the organization cope with uncertainty and its indisputable legitimacy. If these are the *ends*, from here on our interest will be mainly in *means*.

4

MANAGEMENT DEVELOPMENT NEEDS 1: THE ORGANIZATIONAL LEVEL

The method of management development needs analysis I follow here is that of McGehee and Thayer (1961), which Bramley (1992: 9) claims to be 'the most influential text on training needs analysis'. The basis of the McGehee and Thayer method is that needs analysis is required at three levels – organization, job and person – and that unless this three-tiered approach is followed, decisions about interventions are bound to be sub-optimal. There is a compelling logic to this argument, and about the adverse consequences of not following it, some of which I raised in the last chapter.

Take, for example, an organization which bases most of its decisions about management development needs with greatest reference to the needs of individual managers, and too little to job and organization needs. There were findings (Hussey, 1985) that the majority of British organizations used to take just such an approach, and it is my observation that many still do. They live in a world of 'development by menu', where managers are offered an array of courses from which they choose, or are guided to choose, those items which 'suit' them. This may be an outcome of a performance appraisal, or a career development discussion, or even a general enquiry to the training department. The rationale for actually attending such an event can be influenced by factors other than individual learning. I have, over the years, heard various other rationales cited, such as novelty or entertainment value, individuals being offered places on courses to fill places made available through other candidates' withdrawal, and responding to a complaint that an individual has not attended a course for a long time. If these rationales were typical, they would help explain the supply-driven nature of UK management development, as examined in Chapter 2.

At the other end of the spectrum, basing decisions about interventions on organizational needs alone, without regard for job and person needs, can lead to equally absurd outcomes. A common example is the type of programmatic change initiative often introduced to organizations when a vendor of such products, such as a large consulting firm, successfully convinces a chief executive of the merits of a given approach, let us say Business Process Re-engineering (BPR). One of the methods commonly advocated for introducing such an initiative is to train *all* the managers in the organization in the new methodology, top-down, so as to ensure consistency of message. It sounds a plausible tactic, particularly if the approach is purported to be radically different from anything the organization has encountered before. So a training schedule is devised and programmes are run (usually by the consultants who recommend it and at considerable cost) toward the objective of having all managers 'trained' in the ways of righteousness. This approach has been termed – pejoratively but accurately enough – 'sheep-dipping'. One of its greatest failings is that the assumption that the 'new' approach is radically different from anything encountered before turns out often not to be the case.

For one thing, there are always managers who will claim (with some justification) that, having been around for a long time, they have seen all this before. BPR looks, to them, suspiciously like old wine in new bottles – the Work Study, Organization and Methods or Operational Research techniques they can recall being fashionable from the early 1950s to the late 1970s. The Brylcreemed young men with white coats and stopwatches may have given way to assertive 'consultants' in designer suits, but the script feels strangely familiar, pregnant with a 'one best way' sub-plot. Second, it is more than likely that some managers will be genuinely well informed about the proposed change methodology, having read about it, discussed it or even experienced it, perhaps in a different part of the organization or a previous employment. It is also possible that some managers will be better informed about the subject of the intervention than those who are attempting to train them. Finally, there may be a residual cynicism among certain managers, expressed as 'this too shall pass', that senior management has set up many such initiatives in the past, all in a blaze of publicity, most of which faded quite quickly, allowing the *status quo ante* soon to re-establish itself. So when senior managers become excited about their latest initiative, one 'learns' to simulate commensurate excitement, say yes but mean no, collude in the initiative's introduction, and eventually help it die through lack of sustained attention.

Now, if such feelings and attitudes exist among middle and junior managers but, in senior management's rush to introduce programmatic change, these aspects are not surfaced as part of systematic analysis of individual needs, how effective should we expect the 'training' of the middle and junior managers in the change ideology and methodology to be? In a real sense, by holding and sharing such opposing attitudes, they will be 'inoculated' (McGuire 1973: 139) against the attempts to get them to think and behave differently. As Asch (1962: 633) pointed out: 'The areas within which exploitative propaganda is effective are limited. Its force is greatest when people have no direct knowledge or opportunity for direct observation.' Managers at junior and middle levels *do* have direct knowledge of an organization's operations, and the opportunity to observe them not only directly, but at far closer range than senior management can.

All of this offers support for the McGehee and Thayer approach, and the logical starting point is organizational needs. How should they be accessed and analysed? Before attempting to answer that question, it is worth looking at some different perspectives of what organizations are, as these will in turn influence perspectives about their needs.

Concepts of organization

Burrell and Morgan (1979) identify four salient sociological paradigms and related schools of organization analysis: functionalist, interpretive, radical humanist and radical structuralist. They show how each of the four intellectual traditions in sociology has had a corresponding effect on thinking about what organizations are and what they do. We cannot do justice here to the full range and depth of these authors' analysis, but a very simplistic interpretation is that the way one conceptualizes what an organization is affects one's view of how an organization works (its effectiveness) and therefore how to render it more effective. Even within the dominant functionalist paradigm, there is a wide range of concepts of organization, among them: the classical management theorists (some of whose protagonists we met in the last chapter), whose enduring metaphor of organization is a *machine*, to be rendered more efficient; the open systems theorists, whose metaphor of organization is a biological *organism*, pursuing a goal of 'functional unity' (p. 159); the symbolic interactionists, who view organizations as areas of *social action* and who are therefore deeply interested in the 'general orientation of individuals to their roles and with the meaning of work at the subjective level' (p. 195); and the pluralist theorists, who view organizations as areas of *interests, conflict and power*.

Now, these differences in perspective have some obvious consequences for notions of managerial effectiveness and, by implication, for how management should be developed. As we have seen already, the classical model is alive, kicking and highly influential with the management population. This machine model remains an evocative source of engineering thinking and language transferred, analogously, to management behaviour: 'driving change', 'streamlining operations', 'achieving critical mass', 'leveraging relationships'. In the 1990s, the machine model was given a fillip by the emergence and immediate popularity of 're-engineering' (see, for example, Hammer and Champy, 1993). It would be difficult to imagine how an organization could be 're-engineered' unless it were perceived as having similar properties to those of a machine. Where the engineering paradigm is prevalent in management thinking, one can reasonably predict which management behaviours would be valued and which management development approaches would be favoured, and these could be epitomized as 'control'. Here, there will be an emphasis on creating and maintaining order, imposing clear authority, managing tightly against short-term budgets and targets, rigorously measuring performance, rewarding the 'winners' and eliminating the 'losers'. One would also expect management development to be conventional and closely prescribed; at grade *a* the manager attends course *x*, at grade *b* course *y*, and so on.

Contrast this with an organization where an open system thinking is predominant. Here, the behavioural language will draw on biological analogies: 'achieving growth', 'ensuring survival', 'growing successors', 'adapting to the environment' and 'cross-fertilizing knowledge and ideas'. Managers will be cast as guardians of the health of the organism. Their role will be more akin to that of a biochemist or physician than an engineer. For management development, the 'development' part will be construed as a long-term process of individual and collective growth. So one would expect to see less emphasis on laddered courses and more on self-development and use of experiential learning methods. There is a danger here, as there always is with over-played metaphors, of reification – that managers begin to believe that the organization really *is* an organism, which of course it is not, any more than it is a machine. This type of manager will thus be susceptible to anthropomorphic concepts such as 'the learning organization' (which we shall consider more fully in Chapter 7), and imbuing the organization with a 'mind' and even with a 'personality'.

It would be wrong to suggest that all management thinking in any organization is attuned to one particular organizational model or metaphor. Organizations are plural places, where multiple outlooks and agendas both co-exist and conflict. There is also the possibility that ideology, like technology, is contingent on function. Therefore, it is possible to find within a single organization what Burns (1990) terms an *organismic structure* functioning in one location (e.g., where the dominant activity is selling) and a *mechanistic structure* functioning in another (e.g., where the dominant activity is processing). The lesson for those who manage management development should, however, be obvious: it is essential to understand what organizational paradigms are followed in the organization, and where. If, for example, the dominant ideology within the finance function is one of mechanistic control, its managers are likely to be more open to proposals of the conventional short-term training type than those which require long-term experiential learning. This does not, by the way, mean that the latter type of development is necessarily inappropriate; job and person needs analysis might indicate that it is wholly appropriate. But it does mean that greater scepticism or resistance could be expected from finance managers to proposals for experiential learning and that a far greater effort – and probably a great degree of frustration – will be needed to persuade those managers to adopt an unfamiliar approach to their development.

Organizational effectiveness and management

If accurately identifying the presenting organizational paradigm is the first thing, there is a long way to go thereafter in successfully diagnosing where the organization is not meeting its criteria of effectiveness, what action managers should take to achieve greater success and how they should be developed so as to perform those actions more effectively. This is no easy task. As Campbell *et al.* (1970) note:

> Executive behaviour – or, more importantly, *effective* executive behaviour – is a function of complex interactions placed upon persons by the physical, administrative and social environments of their organization, and the nature of the feedback, incentive and reward systems developed by organizational policies and practices.
>
> (1970: 12)

> Managerial effectiveness is more likely than effectiveness in most other jobs to be strongly affected by situational variables.
>
> (1970: 140)

In the face of such difficulties, it would be all too easy to take refuge in 'strategy' – to take an organization's given statement of strategy (if there is one), try to use it to identify what needs to change in order to realize it, find some specific indicators of how management should change, and decide what development might help them change. Storey *et al.* (1997) comment that there is a tendency in UK firms to do just this. For example, a building society may have a stated strategy of becoming, say, 'a broad-based financial services organization', to include banking and insurance activities. If the building society does not yet run banking and insurance operations, it might be an appealing pastime to imagine how its existing managers would successfully run them, and what training they would need to put them in that envious position; appealing, but perhaps futile. If the building society's ambitions can only be realized through acquisition, then it is possible that its existing managers will ultimately have little part to play in banking and insurance. These may be left largely to the managers acquired in the takeovers.

Another problem with an organization's stated strategy (as given to its shareholders in its annual report, or to its employees in a 'vision statement' or 'mission statement') is that it may be too nebulous or bland to allow meaningful constructs of business need, and thereby of management development need, to be operationalized. It may therefore be necessary to gather data from the management population to try to understand how they interpret strategy and the meaning they attach to it as far as their own development is concerned. Take, for example, the following extract from the mission statement of the Co-operative Bank quoted in Williams (1998: 37):

Education and training

To act as a caring and responsible employer encouraging the development and training of all staff and encouraging commitment and pride in each other and the Group.

This sounds highly sensible and commendable but it has to be seen for what it is, which is organizational rhetoric. That does not imply that it lacks sincerity, but it is aimed more at persuading its readers, such as employees and customers, about the qualities and values of the organization rather than stating what the organization actually does. Nevertheless, it does point to certain management development requirements. On the face of it, managers at the Co-operative Bank would need to understand the organization's human resources policies; there appears to be a particular emphasis on fairness and developing others. These might ultimately translate into a management development plan which includes specific attention to recruitment, employee relations, appraisal, career counselling and development planning.

Finally, and crucially, there is a distinct possibility, as observed by Weick (1995), that strategy is constructed *retrospectively*. The building society with broader 'financial services' aspirations may well have already experienced some adventures into banking and insurance: '. . . strategists take credit for their foresight when they are actually trading on their hindsight' (Weick, 1995: 78). So my advice to management development practitioners is not to ignore espoused strategy as a source of directional intent, but to acknowledge its limitations as a framework of analysis for organization-level development needs. A surely more useful tool would be an analytic framework which offers multiple perspectives of organizational effectiveness, and allows the practitioner to select those which appear most relevant and pressing to his or her own organization. I have found no framework more comprehensive than that offered by Schmitt and Klimoski (1991: 236–47), which is summarized in Table 4.1.

Schmitt and Klimoski do not claim this framework to be a typology or taxonomy, but a description of 'general approaches to the definition and measurement of organizational effectiveness'. They offer five perspectives of organizations – goal attainment, open systems, multiple constituency, organization development and human resources accounting – and cite a number of criteria of effectiveness within each of these. They leave it – as do I – to individual readers to decide which perspectives, and within those which criteria, are applicable to their own organizations. However, as I am offering this framework as a device for diagnosing management development needs at the organizational level, one or two examples of how it can be applied might be helpful.

Goal attainment

There are innumerable reasons why an organization's management might fail to attain such goals as profit, productivity, product

Table 4.1 Criteria of organizational effectiveness

Organizational perspective	Criteria of effectiveness
Goal attainment	Profit and profit-related indices Productivity Quality of products or services provided Growth Efficiency
Open systems	Survival Conflict (resolution) Acquisition of resources Flexibility/adaptation Innovation Distinctive competence
Multiple constituency	Satisfaction of multiple stakeholders' requirements and interests, e.g. owners, managers, employees, customers, suppliers, local community, government
Organization development	Leadership processes Motivational processes Communication processes Interaction–influence processes Decision-making processes Control processes
Human resources accounting	Productivity Absenteeism and tardiness Employee turnover Accidents and work-related illnesses (physical and emotional) Grievances, strikes and work stoppages

Source: adapted from Schmitt and Klimoski (1991)

or service quality, growth or efficiency in the short term. Some of these reasons might be entirely outside the control or influence of managers. For example, an oil company's profits might be severely disrupted by a sudden and unexpected conflict in a country where it has extensive drilling operations. However, if management persistently fails to attain its own goals or – more importantly – the goals which are normative in the industry and sector in which it competes – there is every reason to suspect a deficiency in the organization's management capabilities. To under-perform year on year against competitors, whether traditional or emergent, suggests either an enduring inability to comprehend the dynamics of one's environment and the capabilities of one's resources, or, if one does, an unwillingness to do something about it. The vulnerabilities here are, therefore, either poor planning, or insufficiently holding people accountable for results, or both. The management developer needs to be able to distinguish between these problems, since the choice of intervention will depend on that diagnosis. Effective diagnosis relies on an accurate observation and analysis of the symptoms, which may be based on different reports arising out of different interests. Figure 4.1 shows some extracts from a report by a management consultant who has been brought into an organization to investigate why sales targets are not being met.

Let us say that, because the findings appear to suggest that lack of training is a cause of sales under-achievement, the report has been passed to the training manager for comments and recommendations. What should be her response? It is, of course, impossible to draw hard-and-fast conclusions from two small fragments, but we should immediately be able to recognize a possible trap. The information from the management interviews suggests that displacement – 'a word used in psychoanalysis to refer to the shift of focus of emotion from one situation to another' (Evans, 1978: 98) – might be occurring. The managers are attributing the blame for poor sales performance to the underhand behaviour of competitors and lack of self-motivation and skills among their sales staff. Managers, by implication, are not doing anything 'wrong'. (If only our salespeople do more of the same, but with greater skill and energy, things might not be so bad, although our competitors will still conspire to deny us the success we deserve.) So it is down to the training manager to 'fix it' by providing more and better sales training, with a strong 'close that sale' motivational element.

That might be one reading of the situation but there is at least one other, which is offered by the clues in the extracts quoted from

---

Findings

We interviewed 20 of your senior managers to obtain their understanding of the reasons for the non-achievement of sales targets. Their responses fell into two main categories:

(a) *A particularly difficult business environment.* Managers said that margins were being eroded by increasing demands by customers for the provision of peripheral services, but for which customers are unwilling to pay. This problem is exacerbated by the behaviour of your two main competitors, who seem to be prepared to bear losses on peripheral services in order to grow market share at your expense.

(b) *Insufficient self-motivation of sales staff*, possibly linked to insufficient selling skills.

-Page 2-

Appendix 4 – Human resources data

We spent some time with your HR department, who gave us access to some employment statistics. From these it appeared that: the overall level of absenteeism has increased by 20% in the last three years. Among your management and professional grade people it has increased by 42% in the same period. The HR Manager expressed the view that although underlying causes for absenteeism are difficult to pinpoint, he believed an increasing amount of it is 'stress-related'.

-Page 28-

Figure 4.1 Extract from management consultant's report

Appendix 4, buried at the back of the consultant's report. That is that the management of this organization lacks the ability to plan, or to implement plans, or both. Doing 'more of the same' appears to put the firm's employees under increasing strain, and this is particularly marked in the case of professionals. The thing which appears to be missing here is what Sparrow (1994a: 147) calls 'strategic analysis', which he claims:

> ... involves understanding the strategic position of the organization, the environment, resources, values and objectives. Strategic choice involves the formulation of possible

courses of action of options, evaluation of their suitability or fit, and selection of the strategy to be followed. Finally, strategic implementation is concerned with the translation of strategy into action, resource planning, designing the organizational structure to carry through the strategy, and adapting the people and the systems used to manage the organization.

If this is indeed a problem in this organization, and if the training manager recognizes it as such, she is likely to face a difficult time trying to move managers away from their preference for the 'quick fix' of sales training, which would not actually demand their own time, to working on their own longer term development needs. However, there is sufficient 'pain' in the system, in the form of the high absenteeism rates, at least to allow the subject to be broached.

Let us now consider another case, an organization whose goals are realistic, well defined and appropriate, but whose employees in general, and managers in particular, are not held accountable for achieving them. Such an organization could be characterized as being in the land of the permanent project where, rather than confront poor performance, senior managers endlessly constitute, deconstitute and reconstitute project teams around improvement themes such as quality and continuous change. It is almost as though these projects were created as a means of avoiding difficult words and deeds about underperformance, exemplifying Argyris's (1990: 25) contention that:

> Whenever human beings are faced with any issue that contains significant embarrassment or threat, they act in ways that bypass, as best they can, the embarrassment or threat. In order for the bypass to work, it must be covered up.

What better, and superficially sensible, way of covering up than to invent projects with grandiloquent titles and terms of reference, and persuading influential people to join in? It also sounds perfectly reasonable if one claims such projects as being 'developmental' for the people concerned. Other symptoms one might expect to see in such an organization are:

- Executives privately admitting that they 'go along' with demands for them to serve on project teams and steering committees, but find them an annoying distraction from their 'real' jobs.

- Leadership of projects frequently being awarded to executives who are commonly believed to have become ineffective in the roles to which they were appointed or promoted.
- The tendency among senior managers largely to ignore any appraisal scheme in existence. At lower levels, there appears to be a fixation with the bureaucracy of appraisal, such as the design of forms, rather than its possible outcomes for individual performance, development or reward.
- General inattention to evaluation, and the data collection needed to evaluate outcomes effectively. This equally applies to the so-called 'projects' which, after a noisy birth and unremarkable adolescence, begin to wither rapidly for lack of nourishment (e.g. there are more apologies for attendance than attendees at steering committee meetings) and are allowed to die gradually, quietly and, ultimately, without comment.

In such a case, the challenge for the management developer is to identify a development approach which aims to raise the willingness and ability of managers to manage performance, without turning it into yet another doomsday 'project'. It would be all too easy to design and offer performance management training – perhaps tied to the introduction of a new appraisal process – as one of those 'sheep-dip' organization-level interventions mentioned earlier in this chapter. But this problem is concerned with the way that managers confront their own, and one another's, performance. It is more to do with their emotional competence (Schein, 1978) than their ability to understand technique. Argyris has written for a long time, and at length, on this subject (see, e.g., 1962, 1990, 1992). He terms the behaviours which individuals use to avoid confronting one another 'organizational defensive routines' (1992: 84) and defines them thus:

> ... any action or policy that prevents human beings from experiencing negative surprises, embarrassment, or threat, and simultaneously prevents the organization from reducing or eliminating the causes of the surprises, embarrassment and threat. Organizational defensive routines are *anti-learning* and over protective (emphasis added).

For the management developer the problem of anti-learning is twofold. First, if the top team behave that way, they *model* that behaviour to others in the organization, crucially to managers further down the organization. As Bandura (1977b: 192) states:

Because acquisition of response formation is a major aspect of learning, much human behaviour is developed through modeling. From observing others, one forms a conception of how new behaviour patterns are performed, and on later occasions the symbolic construction serves as a guide for action.

In effect, managers learn, all the way down to the bottom of the hierarchy, that 'what counts round here' is not managing performance but willingness to take part in charades called projects, where people talk about, and play at, managing performance.

Second, the management developer must therefore countenance what type of intervention should be used to attempt to change top team behaviour, and to persuade the top team to experience it. There is a strong case here for recommending process consultation, which 'involves a skilled outside consultant working with individuals on groups to help them learn about human and social processes' in which 'the consultant tends to use more non-directive and questioning methods in order to get the group to solve its problems' (Huczynski, 1987: 232). Note that Huczynski assumes an *outside* consultant, and with justification. It is not, in this writer's experience, the type of role which top team members are likely to give willingly to an insider such as the management development manager, and there is evidence that, given the sensitivities of the players, an external consultant can be more effective because s/he is usually assumed to be non-evaluative (Cobb and Margulies, 1989; Walton, 1989).

There remains the issue of persuading the top team to undertake such an intervention. Again, it might not be within the direct range of the management developer's influence actually to do this, and support might need to be obtained from others who do have that influence. A particular problem here – especially if members of the top team have not experienced this type of approach before – is that they may perceive it as a threat both to self-esteem and team (perhaps even organizational) equilibrium, and reject the idea. Ultimately the position taken by the chief executive is likely to be the deciding factor.

These two examples serve to underline a point made in Chapter 2, that to be able to do anything about this type of problem – including diagnosing it effectively – the management developer has to be in an organizational position so to do. This does not necessarily mean having senior status in the corporate hierarchy. By *position* I mean influence rather than direct power. As Beer (1989: 443–6) has pointed out with reference to the success of OD departments, competence and credibility are necessary but not sufficient sources of power; in addition, the management developer needs political access and sensitivity, and sponsorship from a powerful source within the organization.

Open systems

I earlier mentioned the open system perspective, where the dominant metaphor of organization is the living organism, engaged in a struggle for survival, interacting with the environment, importing energy and transforming it into an output (see Katz and Kahn, 1978: 23–4). Although Katz and Kahn are committed and influential protagonists of this approach, they do not shrink from stating the limitations of the model (pp. 30–2): 'Open is not a magic word, and pronouncing it is not enough to reveal what has been hidden in the organizational cave' (p. 33). Let us take one example of organizational need identified by Schmitt and Klimoski, that of innovation. Katz and Kahn identify five types of organizational 'subsystem': production or technical; supportive; maintenance; adaptive; managerial (pp. 51–9). Innovation is quite clearly largely a function of the 'adaptive' subsystem:

> In most formal organizations there arise, therefore, structures that are specifically concerned with sensing relevant changes in the outside world and translating the meaning of those changes for the organization.
>
> (Katz and Kahn, 1978: 55)

How would one detect that, so far as innovation is concerned, the adaptive subsystem is malfunctioning? What sets of factors would be at work in the organization? I suggest some of the following. First, the major sources of new products or services will be things which competitors have already done, or are credited with having done, and which are held to have achieved some degree of success. Second, the 'copies' of products or services are sold at a far lower profit margin than that commanded by the market leader(s). Next, even though there may be a formal research and development function, innovation is not central to the major day-to-day work of the organization. It is something which 'specialists' do, but most other organizational members do not collectively perceive themselves as innovative in outlook. Innovation is not part of their self-identity. Finally, attempts at innovation are, compared to other more familiar activities, half-hearted, and enacted through what Amabile *et al.* (1993: 123) call 'low creativity projects'. (For a comprehensive typology of attributes of innovations, see Wolfe, 1994: 419.)

In summary, the organization is making a poor job of achieving 'environmental constancy by bringing the external world under control' (Katz and Kahn, 1978: 89). Either its managers are not dedicating enough attention and resources to scanning the environment, or are misreading their scans, such that any changes which are being implemented are inadequate or inappropriate. This may be a legacy from a time when the environment was more strongly biased in favour of the organization, furnishing it with results such as abnormal profits. Perhaps the organization's clients were prepared to pay premium prices despite an indifferent quality of the products or services provided, simply because there was a shortage of other, competitive sources of supply. (This might hold true, for example, for British motor manufacturers in the 20 years after the Second World War or the insurance industry as late as the 1980s.)

Whatever the cause, the organization today finds that, far from bringing the external world under control, it is slowly but surely losing the battle against its environment. The reaction of managers might be to 'try everything' (for example, by copying everything their competitors do), or do nothing. In either case, Katz and Kahn (1978: 81) note the possibility that 'either extreme, flexibility or rigidity, is related to organizational morbidity; survival apparently calls for some stability or structure but also some flexibility to meet changing environmental conditions'. The challenge for the management developer is not so much somehow to render all the managers more 'innovative' (although there are, not surprisingly, many training organizations which offer courses to do just that) so much as to create the conditions where innovative thinking is encouraged, nurtured and exploited. I would hypothesize that the major requirement of an intervention in these circumstances is rather to change management attitudes – particularly towards risk – than simply to describe techniques for innovative thinking.

Attitude change is no trivial pursuit. Zimbardo and Ebbesen (1969: 18–20) offer a four-stage process model which suggests that a change in opinion is a combined function of the individual's *initial position*, his/her *attention* to the communicator and the message, *comprehension* of its arguments and *motivation* for accepting its position. Therefore the developer faced with changing attitudes towards risk would be wise to adopt an intervention design which sought to measure and manipulate these four variables. Questions to be asked at the first stage might be:

- What are the prevailing attitudes among managers towards risk and innovation?
- How could we measure them? (Survey? Interviews? Focus groups? Other methods?).
- How could we use the data from those measures to design an intervention? How could we effectively test the design and its effects on attention, comprehension and motivation in a pilot exercise, before applying it to the whole management population?

Conclusions

I hope, from the examples given, to have reinforced my argument that management development should be seen primarily as an instrument of organizational change, and that to achieve that, the management developer has both to comprehend the needs of the organization and *know how* to comprehend those needs. I hope, too, that I have demonstrated that the use of a sound diagnostic framework, such as that offered by Schmitt and Klimoski, is essential to that process. My examples were taken from the goal attainment and open system perspectives, but the approach would apply equally well to multiple constituency, organization development and human resources accounting issues (and indeed some aspects of these were illustrated in our examples). But as we have seen from the Zimbardo and Ebbesen model above, knowledge of a problem is one thing, motivation to do something about it is quite another. Do management developers typically see and position themselves as organizational change agents? There is some evidence (Pettigrew *et al.*, 1982) that only a small minority do, but also that this is changing as organizations more frequently begin to see the possibilities of management development as a 'strategic weapon' (Baldwin and Padgett, 1994: 303). Our examples strongly indicate that change agency is not a soft option for the developer; how much easier to satisfy a short-term management appetite for training activity than invest analytical and conceptual thinking, politicking, persistence and courage into long-term development efforts. For those inclined, or encouraged, to take the more difficult of the two routes, I shall now move on to the next part of the journey.

5

MANAGEMENT DEVELOPMENT NEEDS 2: THE JOB LEVEL

In Chapter 2 I noted the difficulties encountered by researchers trying to pin down what managers do. This chapter will give some guidance in how to analyse what managers do in the particular organizations in which they work, primarily for the purpose of developing them. We should not overlook, however, that *job analysis*, our pinning-down method, has uses other than development, including recruitment and selection, establishing compensation levels, performance appraisal, vocational guidance and succession planning. The logic of job analysis is unassailable. As Greuter and Algera note (1992: 143):

Job analysis should lead to the identification of relevant traits that are necessary for successful job performance. In conducting a job analysis, the job content must not be analysed in a superficial, global way, but a more or less protracted, objective and systematic study of individuals actively engaged in the particular activity is called for.

The problems in analysing managerial jobs, however, while they have long been recognized, have not, apparently, yet been successfully overcome. Campbell *et al.*, writing in 1970, put it this way:

Describing requirements of managerial jobs is unusually

51

difficult because such jobs are subject to so many changes. Any given job or position at the managerial level changes from time to time, from person to person, and from situation to situation . . . What is needed is a set of fundamental dimensions to describe or measure the job behaviours desired at a particular time and for a particular situation.

(Campbell *et al.*, 1970: 99)

More recently, Cascio (1991) says:

Performing an accurate job analysis for any job is not an easy task, but problems are compounded for managerial jobs. Different activities occupy the manager's time, such as planning and organising work or settling disputes among subordinates. Person-determined changes are obvious when two managers at the same level and functional specialty are given similar administrative responsibilities for achieving organizational objectives, but they use widely divergent methods in order to do so. Finally, situation-determined changes also affect managerial jobs in different functional areas, on different hierarchical levels, and in different geographical regions and organizations.

(Cascio, 1991: 209)

The job analysis method I outline here draws particularly on the methodology for accessing competencies, specifically managerial competencies. This does not mean being blind to the controversies and limitations of the competency approach, which we shall presently examine. Moreover, I make no claim for the competency approach other than that it is a job analysis method, and only that, and one of several methods available to practitioners, depending on needs, and the resources available to conduct research (see Pearn and Kandola, 1988, for a thorough review). The particular advantage of the competency method is its suitability for managerial work. As noted above, the analysis of management jobs must somehow meet Greuter and Algera's criteria of being objective and systematic, while trying somehow to span the variability in individual managers' jobs, as noted by Cascio. In other words, it must try to bridge the universal and the particular, and have clear and practical relevance to the organization which uses it. As Sparrow (1994b: 13) observes: 'Individual employee behaviour has to be arranged in the context of organization competencies. Why? Because management skills are increasingly organization-specific.'

Competencies: a mixed blessing?

Boam and Sparrow (1992), in the preface to their book on designing and achieving competency, remark:

> It is not surprising that the appetite of organizations to find out more about 'competency approaches' has grown. Unfortunately, these wonderful tools have been largely the preserve of individual academics and consultants. Perhaps as a result, there seems to have been a perfect negative correlation between the increasing interest and published work on 'competency approaches' and the level of confidence that managers have in writings of the experts.

Since the publication of that extract there appears to have been a substantial increase in interest in the competency approach by UK organizations, based, for example on the number of conferences annually given to it, magazine articles, and indeed the appearance of a journal dedicated to the subject. It certainly seems that having a 'competency framework' is becoming *de rigueur* among human resources departments, and a growing number of large organizations claim to have one (du Gay *et al.*, 1996). In short, competencies have become fashionable. It has taken some time for this to happen; the acknowledged seminal work on this subject, Boyatzis's *The Competent Manager,* was published in 1982. A reasonable question is whether competencies are yet another management panacea which is now having its day. Gill and Whittle (1993: 289) identify four stages in the life cycle of a management panacea: 'birth' – which lasts 10 years, and which begins when the 'inventor/charismatic leader writes seminal books'; a further 10-year 'adolescence' ('consultants/senior managers promote the packaged invention'); a 10-year period of 'maturity' ('routinized/bureaucratized by consultants and internal staff'); and 'decline', which starts after about 30 years, where costs begin to exceed apparent benefits. If we were to apply the Gill and Whittle model to competencies, we could reasonably conclude that the birth is long over and we are somewhere between adolescence and maturity.

There are now examples of 'how to identify competency' methodologies (see Kandola and Pearn, 1992; Spencer and Spencer, 1993). A number of consulting firms offer their services to help organizations access and apply competencies. So it is quite possible by now that many more managers have confidence in the competency concept than they had in 1982 or, to put it another way, competencies now enjoy greater face validity among managers. But, if we dig deeper, can practitioners now have absolute confidence that competencies are well supported by relevant theory, and by a body of evidence from appropriate empirical studies? The answer to both questions is still no. Boyatzis himself (1982: 9) drew attention to possible limitations of the approach.

Criticism of the competency approach has since come from many quarters and in various guises: for its narrowness and over-simplification (Jacobs, 1989); for its placing too much emphasis on current indications of successful performance and not enough on future indicators (Cockerill, 1989); for having too strongly a technocratic orientation (Reed and Anthony, 1992). There have also been semantic arguments about differences between the words *competence* and *competency* (see Woodruffe, 1992: 17). And even where the word 'competency' is used, we find different meanings associated with it. Some organizations follow Woodruffe (1992: 17) in seeing a competency as: 'the set of behaviour patterns that the incumbent needs to bring to a position in order to perform its tasks and functions with competence'.

Other organizations, such as those who have adopted the Hay McBer consultancy's approach (see, e.g., Spencer *et al.*, 1992), would view Woodruffe's definition as describing a *threshold* competency, and prefer to try to understand what aspects of an individual's performance differentiate it as superior to the average. Such organizations tend to follow the Spencer and Spencer (1993: 9) definition of competency as: 'an underlying characteristic of an individual that is causally related to criterion-referenced effective and/or superior performance in a job or situation'.

Finally, as Williams (1998: 114) points out, there is another way of drawing two distinct meanings from the word 'competency': one which 'places emphasis on the personal attributes which underlie behaviour – what people are' and a second which 'concentrates on the clusters of related behaviour, that is, what people do' – in other words, there are both *content* and *process* notions of competency. It is helpful to follow Williams's (p. 126) advice in viewing competency as 'a middle-order variable of some kind – that is, clusters of behaviour signifying some syndrome of personal characteristics . . . that are required to achieve some defined level of output'.

If the conceptual basis of competency is unclear (and, from the above, it looks like an arena for metaphysical argument) there is also little in the way of convincing empirical support for the effects of competency approaches on organizational effectiveness, other than the usual crop of 'we did this and it worked for us' anecdotes, of the type found in the more lightweight human resources publications. The effect of competencies on management development in particular, from such evidence as exists, looks no better than equivocal (Antonacopolou and Fitzgerald, 1996). So why bother with competencies at all? I return to my earlier point that the competency approach should be considered no more than one of several methods of job analysis, and job analysis is but a means to an end (or several ends), never an end in itself. I also suggested that the competency approach might have a particular advantage when it comes to analysing management work, with all its inherent variability. My own experience of this has been positive, and in the Appendix I describe a piece of research undertaken to access and use competencies in one organization. This provides the interested practitioner with some guidance on methodology for identifying competencies, and how, once identified, they can provide the basis for management development planning.

From the results of the research it would not be unreasonable to conclude that the study organization has, through the development and application of managerial competencies as a job analysis method, appeared to bring some utility and, indeed, integration to its human resource practices, particularly in the area of management development. Arguably, it could have obtained this utility from *any* job analysis method, to some degree or another. Are there any distinctive benefits of the competency method over other job analysis methods, or is it merely old job analysis wine in new bottles? The probable truth is that to a great extent it is very much like old wine. Conceptually, it follows what Cascio calls the 'behavioural content' approach to the study of managerial work, seeking answers to the question 'what common behaviours do managers engage in as they carry out their jobs?' (1991: 211). And we should heed Cascio's warning, based on his reading of research by Whitely (1985), 'not to over-generalise based on similarities in managerial work behaviour, for managerial jobs differ in terms of demands, constraints and choices ... The challenge now is to discover the linkages between managers' personal qualities, behavioural requirements of their jobs, and measures of organizational success' (p. 213). To do what Cascio asks, even for one single organization, requires patient, rigorous, longitudinal research, and that is something which is currently absent, but may emerge in time. Meanwhile, if senior managers such as those in the study organization are able to relate more readily to the concepts and language of 'competency' than other forms of job analysis, it is likely that the 'competency movement' will continue to gain momentum. It is also likely that the more thoughtful among management development practitioners will be able to take advantage of this phenomenon to improve management development practice in their organizations.

Returning to job analysis in general rather than competencies in particular, it is worth re-emphasizing how fundamental this process is to the integration of development and other human resources activities. Figure 5.1 is an adaptation of a schematic from an organization where job analysis, in the form of competency model development, provides the underpinning conceptual framework for all the main HR practices.

Taking each element in turn:

Job analysis

This organization has identified four main job families, including management, and identified a competency model for each. Every employee's job can be categorized into one of these four families.

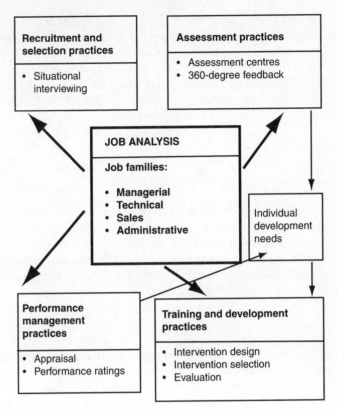

Figure 5.1 Relationship between job analysis and human resources practices

The competency models state, for each constituent competency (such as 'Concern for quality') the behaviours and characteristics of superior performers. There is a five-point rating scale for each competency.

Recruitment and selection

The organization has developed a set of recruitment protocols for each of the four job families. Anyone wishing to hire a manager, for example, has recourse to a template of competencies – such as achievement orientation, conceptual thinking and change leadership – which are deemed to be important to *any* managerial role in the organization. There is also a set of situational interview questions, each designed to seek evidence of particular competencies, which can be used to construct a standard interview process for each candidate. Any other specific knowledge, skills or ability requirements for the role may be assessed by using supplementary interview questions, biodata, tests, work samples or combinations of these.

Assessment

In a similar way to recruitment, competencies provide the basis of the design of assessment tests and exercises for managerial and other roles. They also predicate the design of the organization's 360-degree feedback instruments. The outcomes of assessment centres and 360-degree feedback form the basis for the construction of individual development feedback and planning.

Performance management

Job analysis has been found to be a particularly useful adjunct to the appraisal process in focusing on development needs which, if met, could be expected to lead to more effective achievement of objectives. Discussion about competencies and how to enhance them is likely to be far more productive than the sterile question: 'What courses have you attended recently?'

Training and development

This has been perhaps the field of activity which has benefited most from job analysis, for a number of reasons. First, it has been possible to base the criteria for interventions very specifically on the competency requirements of the various job families. So, for example, programmes have to be purposefully put together to attempt to increase levels of proficiency in given competencies. Typically, these programmes have a primary competency purpose, such as increasing the individual's ability to influence others or to manage change, but are usually designed to raise levels of ability in other competencies which are related, within jobs, to the primary purpose. So a programme labelled 'Achieving Business Impact' has as its main purpose increased effectiveness in the competency called 'Impact and Influence', but also seeks to develop competencies called 'Achievement Orientation' and 'Concern for Quality'. Having specified the purpose of the intervention in this way, the design can be fleshed out and a provider selected. This process stands in marked contrast to the passive 'off-the-shelf' purchasing of training and development, often done on a questionable basis (such as going along with current fashion, or yielding to sales pressure from a supplier), which used to prevail in this organization, and prevails still in many others.

The second main benefit is that there is now a very clear linkage between development need, as identified from performance management and assessment processes, and the intervention actually selected for the individual. I shall have more to say about this in the next chapter, but for now I make the obvious statement that one stands a better chance of finding something if one knows what one is looking for. Managers no longer have to fumble to identify the development needs problem, and then fumble some more to find a solution. Job analysis helps direct them, by describing behaviours, to the problem and the possible solutions, and it does it quickly, especially with practice. Finally, job analysis offers the only realistic route towards effective evaluation of development interventions. To state the obvious once again, one has to understand what a job is in order to understand whether its incumbent is performing more effectively after a development intervention than before it.

Perhaps the final puzzle here is why I should feel the need to keep stating the obvious about job analysis, a technique which can be traced back at least as far as 1911, according to Greuter and Algera (1992). I have seen many general texts on human resources and found that job analysis is mentioned more often than not, so most practitioners are probably aware of it. Perhaps it is seen as requiring too much effort, or being too difficult, or as not being valued, or even as not being relevant. It does require some effort to do job analysis well but it is not excessively difficult and, as shown in this chapter and the Appendix, it can be of enormous value and relevance to management development work.

6

MANAGEMENT DEVELOPMENT NEEDS 3: THE INDIVIDUAL LEVEL

So far, I have tried to create the impression that identifying management development needs at the organization and job levels is no trivial task. The reader should therefore be warned that the identification of needs at the individual level is probably the most difficult piece of the three-stage analysis, in my experience. Once we enter the world of the individual, we enter a world of individual differences. Consider, for a moment, the range of variables which could affect an individual manager's capacity or predisposition to be developed. To name just a few, we might suggest: motivation, age, level of experience, cognitive ability, education and training to date, social values, social pressures (such as those from the manager's immediate family) and state of physical health. We might add to those some factors which the manager 'has' because of his/her current organizational circumstances. Some examples might be:

- The manager's boss has a belief that the only way to learn is as he did, 'the hard way', and that all formal programmes are a waste of the organization's money.
- The manager is located in an overseas office and is out of the

normal range of consciousness of the central human resources
function that arranges most of the management development
activities.

- The manager is three years from retirement and there is an
  unwritten rule that nobody with less than five years to go
  before retirement should be selected for formal development
  programmes.
- Budget cuts have just been announced and no formal development programme is to be sanctioned for any manager for the
  next two years.

All too often, the complexity of the individual factors at play in
trying to decide what interventions might be appropriate is over-
looked. There is a clamour from senior management for a 'toolbox' of development solutions to suit all situations. If executive a
is in age range b, has c years' experience in performing role d and
has previously attended courses e and f, then it is time for her to
attend the two-week residential programme g. The clamour is
understandable, and difficult to resist. Surely, runs the question,
deciding what piece of development somebody should 'do' next
cannot be that difficult? As I showed in the last chapter, it is a lot
easier with the help of sound job analysis, but it is not mechanical.
It would be interesting to ask the 'toolbox'-orientated managers
how they would react if, on visiting their general practitioner, they
were asked very little about the particular ailments from which
they were suffering, but hastily offered a choice from the two or
three current best-selling medications available.

Clearly, there is a need to limit the range of development
options made available in organizations; sheer practicality and
cost-effectiveness dictate this. But this does not have to mean that
one's approach to management development should be akin to
that of dipping sheep. The closer the understanding that the
management development practitioner can achieve of the individual manager's needs, expectations, attributes and circumstances, together with an understanding of the needs of the
organization and the job, the nearer will s/he be to a useful and
meaningful intervention. This is perhaps the true art of the successful management developer: the ability to diagnose needs in
such a way that the specific development activities recommended

to the individual manager provide optimal outcomes for the manager, the job and the organization. But is this realistic? Might the temptation to represent this hypothetical congruence – perhaps in the form of that old cliché of three overlapping circles beloved by trainers everywhere – be misguided? Let us look at some of the more common methods of accessing management development needs at the individual level.

The appraisal process

Appraisal or – more fashionably – *performance appraisal*, as an element of *performance management* (see Williams, 1998: 1–32), has been around since at least the 1920s (Fletcher and Williams, 1992: 5). Typically, it takes the form of a one-to-one interview, usually annually, between an individual and that individual's immediate supervisor, that is, the person who has the major interest in and responsibility for the individual's tasks, goals, rewards and future development. In the past, such a supervisor was characteristically referred to as the individual's *line manager*, but this term has begun to lose some currency in recent years with the advent of more fluid, or more ambiguous, power structures in organizations such as matrix- and project-based forms. Dulewicz and Fletcher (1992: 652–3) identify seven purposes for performance appraisal: performance review, work planning, basis for compensation and benefits, identification of training and development needs, transfer and promotion potential, identification of long-term potential, succession and career planning. Clearly, the last four are all related to development. Conceivably then, if appraisal is capable of performing these different functions, it represents a rich source for identifying and satisfying the development needs of individual managers. What better way of surfacing these needs than a full and frank discussion between the manager and his or her supervisor? According to the conventional wisdom of appraisals, this regular, institutionalized employee–supervisor dialogue is of great developmental value and, if carried out well, offers some clear benefits.

First, the person doing the appraising is accountable for the performance of the person being appraised, and it is therefore in the appraiser's interests for the person appraised to perform more effectively. One way of achieving more effective performance from the appraisee, arguably, is first to provide him or her with honest feedback about performance deficiencies, and then to attempt to provide the knowledge, skill or motivation to over-come these deficiencies through some form of developmental intervention. Thus, so this argument goes, if the appraiser – let us say, a senior general manager – recognizes that one of her sub-ordinate managers is under-achieving in relation to the goals set for him because of ineffective interpersonal behaviour towards peers and those reporting to him, that general manager will have good reason to use the appraisal interview to confront and explore the problems with the subordinate and agree an appropriate course of action to address them. So the general manager might recommend some form of programme aimed at improving the individual's ability to listen, and respond appropriately, to others, and reinforce this with monitoring the behaviour of the subordi-nate, perhaps giving feedback and coaching whenever inadequate interpersonal skills are observed, or reported by others.

Second, the person doing the appraisal is usually the person who holds the training and development budget required to pay for the appraisee's development, so there is a logic to the appraisal not only identifying development needs, but being used to plan development activity so as to fit in with the budgetary require-ments of the department concerned. And because the appraiser is responsible for all the people reporting to him or her, s/he can use the appraisal process to set priorities about individual interven-tions, and schedule interventions in a way which reduces disrup-tion to the department concerned, for example by ensuring that two departmental managers do not attend the same training course at the same time.

Finally, there is value in tracking development needs over time, and because the appraisal is usually an annual fixture it provides a regular opportunity for the appraiser to monitor the effects of previous development interventions as well as to consider new ones. This feature of appraisal, if carried out well, can be a par-ticularly useful one. Let us suppose that at last year's appraisal, a junior manager was found to have been unsuccessful at perform-ing certain objectives owing to lack of knowledge of the work processes which immediately preceded and followed those which she was managing. The appraiser suggested that the manager should be assigned to each of the two departments (A and B) concerned for a period of a month. At this year's appraisal, the appraiser and junior manager agree that there has been a marked improvement in the flow of work between her department and the one which follows in the process (B), but that problems are still being experienced with the department whose work precedes (A). On questioning, the appraiser is reminded that the period of a month scheduled for the manager's assignment to Department A was cut to a week because of staff sickness in her own department, and it is agreed that a further three weeks' assignment should be arranged as soon as possible. The connection between underperformance and missed development is made, a reasonable cause-and-effect hypothesis formed and remedial action taken. Arguably, the chances of this happening would have been greatly reduced had the annual appraisal not taken place.

We may conclude, then, that appraisal offers an effective means of identifying management development needs at the individual level. As always, that conclusion would need to be qualified. Certainly, appraisal *could* be effective if a number of conditions were met, for example:

- The appraiser is trained not just in the appraisal process, but also specifically in how to identify development needs. S/he is also aware of what development methods are available, and able to distinguish what is available from what would actually be suitable.
- The appraisee is open to the idea that some form of development could improve his or her performance and potential for advancement into a senior role, and is prepared to accept the appraiser's guidance in trying to find a suitable development approach.
- The surrounding organization is supportive of the process. For example, the appraiser's boss does not overturn the appraiser's recommendations by claiming that, although there is a budget provision for them, they are 'too expensive', or that 'the timing is not right'. Also, that the appraisee is reinforced by the reactions

of others (particularly of peers) to the proposed development; that peers do not, for instance, undermine the proposals by statements such as 'Well, I did that course five years ago and it was a complete waste of time.'

These conditions are not always met. Appraisal is often presented as an all-purpose event, combining performance review with development needs, but it can suffer from a general reluctance by managers to carry out appraisals, as observed by Dulewicz and Fletcher (1992: 658):

Napier and Latham (1986) found that many managers saw little or no practical value in conducting appraisals, regardless of whether the feedback given to subordinates is primarily favourable or unfavourable. Given that kind of jaundiced but not unreasonable view, one can hardly be surprised that appraisals are not taken seriously or are avoided altogether. For the majority of managers, they are a high-risk activity with little tangible reward. Organizations frequently pay lip service to the importance of developing subordinates, but little beyond that. The consequence of not carrying out appraisals is more often than not a deafening silence.

This comment certainly chimes with my own experience from a number of organizations, and probably with many of the practitioners who are reading this. Appraisal is much like being faced with boiled cabbage when you are a child; no matter how much people tell you how good it is for you, you just *know* you will never enjoy it. Yet even if the appraising manager is enthusiastic about the process, there remains the question of his or her competence to identify development needs accurately. As Fletcher and Williams (1992: 27) put it:

The principal means of identifying training and development needs appears to be the appraisal scheme. The training and development section of the report form ought to have a broad purpose, and contain specific comments on what is required: it is not sufficient to say something like 'needs to attend a management training course' because such a statement is far too vague. Appraisal information which is of poor quality, and of insufficient quantity, reduces the ability of the training function to respond appropriately.

Unfortunately then, it seems that the considerable potential of appraisal to help develop managers, or any other employees, is often lost. Managers need to learn, and management developers need to help them to learn, that developing others is about exploring individual needs rather than rushing to prescribe pre-existent 'remedies'. Nicholson and West (1988: 43) make this comment:

> We do find that managerial jobs are by and large need-fulfilling, but it seems that organizations are often judged to be inadequate in what they do to help managers. Recognition for achievement, feedback, opportunities for advancement, and learning opportunities, are often insufficient, and, subsuming these, the quality of top management is judged to be deficient. It would seem that for many managers the satisfactions they are able to extract from work are by virtue of their autonomous efforts and not through the supportive agency of well-designed human resource systems . . .

My difficulty is that, while the rationale of appraisal as a tool for management development is unassailable, I wonder whether it will ever actually deliver its promise to the general population of managers.

360-degree feedback

This technique, sometimes termed 'multi-rater' feedback, attempts to overcome some of the limitations of conventional appraisal by using a number of sources to rate an individual's current level of performance or development against some predetermined criteria. These sources will normally include the individual's self-rating, that of the individual's immediate boss, and those of subordinates, peers, superiors (i.e., those senior to the person being rated, but not that person's immediate boss) and others such as clients. The technique is not new; IBM incorporated a subordinate appraisal system in its annual employee survey in the early 1960s, when subordinates were asked to provide feedback to their managers on their performance (Bernardin, 1996). In recent years, however, the usage of this form of feedback in organizations has grown to the point of becoming, according to Moses *et al.* (1993: 294) a 'popular fad'. Advocates of the technique claim a number of advantages for it over conventional one-to-one feedback methods. Bernardin (1996: 432–3), for example, cites eight such advantages of 360-degree feedback as it relates specifically to the assessment of managers. He argues that, if properly implemented, it provides: a valid source of assessment for 'certain managerial dimensions' (i.e., competencies); useful feedback to managers; reinforcement of good managerial behaviour; enhancement of employees' feeling that they have a voice in organizational decision making; facilitation of group changes; greater attention to subordinate needs; a more practical and efficient method of assessment than other procedures (e.g., assessment centres); enhancement of the recruitment process of non-managerial professionals.

There is empirical support for some of Bernardin's propositions. Hazucha *et al.* (1993) undertook a longitudinal study of 48 managers, who with 150 other raters completed a 360-degree instrument at Time 1, and two years later (Time 2) completed it again, together with a questionnaire about perceptions of what development had occurred for the 48 managers – factors such as advancement, effort made, change and development activities such as training. From this they concluded that 360-degree feedback was, overall, an effective management development tool, and that management skills were (or, perhaps more accurately *perceived* to be) important to advancement. McEvoy and Beatty (1989) carried out a seven-year study of ratings of 60 law enforcement agency managers. In this, ratings from assessment centres and by subordinates in Year 1 were compared with ratings by subordinates, ratings by supervisors and promotions in Years 3, 5 and 7. They found that subordinate ratings were 'considerably better intermediate term predictors of ratings than the O(verall) A(ssessment) (R)atings (i.e., those obtained from assessment centres), but the latter "caught up" in predictive power in the long term (actually surpassed, but the differences were not statistically significant)' (p. 50). Their conclusion was that 'if an organization is looking for a prediction approach for up to seven years into the future, subordinate ratings may be as effective as assessment centres and certainly less expensive' (pp. 50–1).

However, there are, as might be expected, some dissenting voices. Moses *et al.* (1993) claim that 360-degree feedback 'relies on instruments designed to capture information from a variety of sources in the hope that the feedback from these sources can best be applied by the individual. While (we) applaud the idea of collecting information from a variety of sources, the overall simplicity of the information collection process limits the usefulness of the information' (p. 294). They argue that, rather than basing ratings on other people's *opinions* of the person being rated, we would do better to base them on other people's *expectations* (OPEs), '. . . the aggregated accumulation of a series of opinions which are held by others concerning a future performance outcome' (p. 286). Furthermore: 'While many 360-degree feedback instruments provide the potential for some form of feedback, only OPE feedback provides the individual with an *opportunity to manage the expectations of others*' (pp. 294–5, original emphasis). Arguably, the position taken by Moses *et al.* is not contrary to 360-degree feedback in principle; rather it is concerned with the type of instrumentation which should be used. In my own experience, this is a legitimate concern. Even after all the conventional wisdom about 360-degree feedback has been taken into account, such as guaranteeing the anonymity of raters, having a sufficiently large sample of raters and processing feedback questionnaires in good time, there remain serious methodological problems related to the questionnaire design and its psychometric properties (Fletcher *et al.*, 1998), and to process.

It is the issue of poor process which can bring 360-degree feedback into discredit most quickly, and this should be of concern to the management developer, given that management development is cited as a salient application of 360-degree feedback (Redman and Snape, 1992; IDS, 1995). What does poor process look like? Here are some symptoms, drawn from experience:

- The questionnaire items are too long and convoluted.
- Questionnaire items are based more on attribution, for example about traits, than on explicit, observable behaviours.
- Questionnaire instructions are poorly expressed.
- There is inadequate control of the physical handling of questionnaires, for example to ensure that all or sufficient raters

chosen by the appraisee have returned them in the time allotted (and been chased if necessary), or that the questionnaires have been processed.

These problems are all mechanical, but their incidence quickly begins to lose the trust of those using 360-degree feedback. At a deeper level there is the problem of interpretation of the feedback data, both by the person being rated and his or her supervisor. By interpretation, I mean not only understanding the data as presented in the feedback report, but also how to use the data to generate thinking about possible development needs. If 360-degree feedback is used in the context of a development programme, where those running it have been trained in its use and interpretation, this is less likely to be an issue. But what about the lay line manager who has not had such training? Indeed, is it wise to introduce development based on 360-degree feedback if the line managers have *not* been thoroughly trained? It is unlikely, once a 360-degree feedback programme has been introduced for a large number of managers, that the management development function can handle the job of integrating the data and recommending development actions for all of them, nor is it necessarily desirable. Unfortunately, such issues can begin to emerge *after* the 360-degree feedback process has started to be implemented in the organization. If that happens, the management development function may end up spending a very large amount of time 'putting out fires', rather than evaluating the outcomes of the exercise and using the results to assess common development needs. 360-degree feedback has proved to be a sound method of identifying the individual development needs of managers, as we have seen, but its introduction has to be carefully planned and prepared, particularly in giving managers a thorough understanding of its usage, and ensuring that the mechanics of the system are sound.

Assessment centres

A description is given in the Appendix of how assessment was used in one particular organization to identify individual development needs, as part of the introduction of a senior succession planning process. Assessment centres have been used in organizational settings since the 1950s, although they have their origins in officer selection in Germany before the Second World War (Feltham, 1992: 404). Their use is not restricted to development, as they are also often used for selection, both in hiring in from outside the organization or promoting from within. The distinctive features of assessment centres are that they are short – typically two to three days – and use multiple methods to rate the current performance of participants against predictors of successful performance in the organization. The predictors should be grounded in criteria of successful performance in the organization. Let us suppose that one of these criteria is innovation; that conclusions have been arrived at in the organization, based on collection and analysis of data, that its performance in relation to competitors is strongly associated with its ability to research and develop successful new products. Further research, let us say using the competency methodology described in the last chapter, has found an association between innovation and job performance, and identified that superior job performance appears to be causally related to certain individual characteristics and behaviours. For argument's sake, let us say that successful innovation appears to be related most strongly to two main variables: propensity to share knowledge and ability to evaluate the preliminary results of research projects. If it were decided to set up an assessment centre to attempt to rate how 'good' individuals are (or could be) at doing these things, how might we do it? And, equally – perhaps more – importantly, from a management development standpoint, how could we use the data obtained from this rating to develop the competencies of individuals?

In asking these questions, we are really asking about *predictors.* What tests or exercises should we use so as to make a valid prediction of the actual performance of the individual in the job setting and, crucially for the management developer, of what development interventions would improve performance in the job setting? While the first question has been the subject of much research and writing (see, e.g., Guion, 1989: 119–24), there is rather less guidance available on the second question. Pursuing our relatively simple example above for the moment, let us suppose that those responsible for assessing knowledge sharing and project evaluation competencies establish the assessment centre design shown in Figure 6.1:

Competency

Predictor	Knowledge sharing	Project evaluation
Project case study		•
Leaderless discussion	•	
Structured interview	•	•

Figure 6.1 Example of a simple assessment centre design

Note that, even in this simplistic (and unrealistic) example, one important principle of assessment – that each variable being assessed should be rated using at least two different exercises – has been followed. Let us now suppose that a number of people are assessed using these methods, and rated on each of these two competencies on, say, a five-point scale, where 0 indicates either that the competency was not observed or contra-indicated, and 4 indicates superior performance, and little need for future development. 3 would represent a slight development need, 2 a greater but probably moderate need, and 1 or 0 a more urgent development need. Some account may have to be taken of experience. If a group of senior managers is assessed, then perhaps normative scores of 3 or 4 may be expected; less experienced managers may be expected to have a normative score of Level 1 or 2.

However, pursuing our example, imagine that a senior manager has just been assessed, and rated at Level 1 on both competencies. Those responsible for the assessment have assured themselves, having by now collected data from a large number of centres, that the exercises are sound, and reliably discriminate different levels of competency. They are also confident about the rating scales, that those who observed the exercises were properly trained in the exercise content and the rating scales, and about the procedures followed at the centre. The procedures, they feel, go as far as they can to reduce error or bias by standardizing the way the exercises are briefed to participants and run, and ensuring that

71

observers' ratings of individuals' competencies are rigorously challenged at the evaluation session which follows the exercises. So now somebody – perhaps the management development manager – must give the senior manager feedback about the ratings and explore what they might mean for her development.

As for 360-degree feedback, the results of assessment can often be disturbing for the individual being assessed, especially if s/he has not been assessed before. For reasons which I explored above when looking at appraisal, it is quite probable that the senior manager in this case has not received any type of critical feedback from her boss, or anybody else, for a long time. She may be resentful that her boss has even thought it necessary for her to be assessed. So the initial feedback session, which may be the most potentially developmental experience that manager has received, or will receive, needs to be approached with careful planning and sensitivity. It is important that the person giving the feedback has, before the meeting, marshalled all salient data from the exercises so as to be able to play back specific, accurate examples of what the manager said or did during the exercises which led to the observer rating her performance at Level 1. Note that, although this appears to take a courtroom approach towards evidence, it is not to prove the individual 'guilty'. Rather, it follows the guidance of experienced practitioners such as Feltham (1992: 417) that feedback is more useful the more specifically it focuses on actual observed behaviour. It may be helpful too, at this stage, to obtain some biographical data about the participant, such as her career history and what training and development she has already had. Some of these data will allow the management developer to formulate some early hypotheses about what type of development could now be appropriate.

It would not be unusual for the participant, when confronted with the feedback data, to deny the validity of the method ('How could you possibly reach that conclusion from a half-hour exercise?' or make excuses ('I wasn't feeling well that day') (Witkowski and Stiensmeier-Pelster, 1998). In our experience, it is not usually helpful for the person giving feedback to respond to such criticism by vigorously defending the methodology used. It is more productive to feed back exactly what was observed. For example, based on the evidence of knowledge sharing from the leaderless discussion group exercise, observations fed back might be as follows:

- 'Although your brief contained important product information which could have been useful to the group's decision process, you did not reveal any of it during the meeting.'
- 'On at least four occasions you were observed to cut short someone's attempt to contribute information by talking over them.'

In my experience, persistent refusal by a participant to accept feedback, or accept the process on which it is based, does occur, but very rarely. The majority of people being assessed for development purposes do seem to want to take note of data which could be useful to their own development and, ultimately, their careers. So as the feedback interview continues, the reviewer should patiently and thoroughly present the data to the participant, allowing space for questioning, discussion and reflection. It is vital that this process is not largely one-way, like the delivery of a school report. As the interview unfolds, the interviewer should be encouraging response from the participant, particularly on what s/he sees as the development needs and how they could be addressed. These responses also provide a further source of data for the reviewer to test the hypotheses made before the interview about what development interventions might be suitable.

This interview is not a coaching session, nor is it a counselling session, though it may have elements of these. It is fundamentally a diagnostic session, and perhaps not unlike a clinical consultation in purpose, if not style and content. It should be clear that anyone conducting such a session needs to be thoroughly competent to do it. This is in great part a matter of training, but it may also be a matter of temperament, in my experience. It requires a level of detachment by the reviewer to avoid emotional engagement and identification with the issues of the interviewee. Some people find this difficult to do, since they display behaviour which Geis and Christie (1970), from their research on how people perform in interactions, characterize as 'low Mach(iavellian)', for example: '. . . low Machs' more personal, open orientation makes them less effective as strategists in the course of interaction, but more sensitive to others as individual persons' (p. 312). This is not meant to imply the opposite, that to be effective at giving feedback one needs to be highly Machiavellian. But it does perhaps help explain why feedback often seems to be better received when it is offered by a disinterested party, such as an independent occupational psychologist, than from someone very familiar with the person being assessed.

Towards the end of the interview, some tentative conclusions should have been aired by both parties about possible future development actions, and evaluated for their practicality as far as the participant is concerned. Let us suppose, for example, in the case of our senior general manager, that she has agreed the need to work on her knowledge-sharing and project-evaluation competencies. The question now is how she might do this. Taking knowledge sharing first, which is perhaps concerned more with her outward behaviour, some opportunity has to be sought which will allow her to learn and practise such behaviour. As we shall see in the next chapter, modelling can be particularly useful here, so who might provide a model to this manager? It needs to be someone with whom the manager comes into frequent contact, and who is seen as successful and effective by that manager. It could be useful here to provide some examples of very competent behaviour (based on the rating scale) and ask the manager what people she knows who display them. Could she perhaps be assigned, even as an observer, to a project team which is led by such a person? Would that person be willing to act as a coach for her? (The chances are that, if that person were an effective sharer of knowledge, he or she would show a strong willingness to act as a coach, which might of itself serve to reinforce the message.)

Project evaluation competency presents a different challenge, since it may require the learning of some specific knowledge, for example of the heuristics which more effective managers use when they make judgements about project feasibility. This naturally raises the question of whether that knowledge has been captured during the competency research. (If not, the illustration serves to emphasize a point made in the last chapter about the near worthlessness of poorly operationalized competency descriptions.) If it has been captured, then the management development function may have designed a formal programme to impart that knowledge, or have located external sources (for example, the social science faculty of a university which can offer teaching in research methodology) which can do it. Before the meeting is concluded, there should at least be some commitment to exploring these development options. The person being assessed then needs to take the dialogue forward with her boss, so that commitment is built up for the forward programme of action and, if necessary, approval is gained for any expenses which might be incurred in realizing these objectives. Finally, and crucially, there needs to be some monitoring process established, first to ensure that the actions are actually taken, and second, to assess their effectiveness over time. If conventional appraisal and/or 360-degree processes are in place, they could serve a useful purpose here.

From the above it should be clear that assessment, if done well, is a potent source of individual needs analysis, and that assessment feedback can be a particularly fruitful means of developing managers, and others. Are there any disadvantages? Perhaps the major one is cost. Compared with conventional appraisal or 360-degree feedback, the cost per person of assessment centres is very high indeed.

There is no point in even considering assessment unless there has been a thorough analysis of managerial jobs, using competencies or some other methodology. A great deal of thought must be given to the selection and design of appropriate assessment centre tests and exercises. It is no argument to suggest that, because old war-horses like the 'in-tray exercise' have worked in numerous organizational settings, they should work for you, regardless of what competencies you are seeking to develop. Beware, also, those practitioners (particularly consultants) who bring their own box of toys with them and implore you to use a particular exercise because 'it's very helpful'. Very helpful to whom? Assessment centres are expensive: their design needs to be as parsimonious as you can possibly make it. So you cannot afford extra baggage, particularly when it is in the form of the comfort blankets or totems of particular practitioners. The design of exercises, such as case studies and role plays, is not a task for amateurs, and it costs time and effort to produce valid material.

Having developed the tests and exercises, there is then the cost of training people to be observers at the assessment centres. But before training, there is the job of selecting them. The conventional wisdom is that observers should be selected from the general management population. After all, general managers should know what they are looking for. Some caution needs to be exercised here, if only because my own experience of this has been mixed. Recall that every effort should be made to minimize sources of error and bias, to which we might add *attributed* sources of error and bias. If an individual considers the results of an assessment centre to be 'bad', in the sense that they threaten to damage his or her self-esteem, that person might attribute his or her low ratings to the bias of a particular observer or observers, perhaps because they have worked for or with them in the past.

In one case with which I am familiar, an experienced senior executive accepted the role of observer, was fully trained and duly acted as an observer at senior level assessment centres. This observer followed all the rules of evaluation, citing only behavioural evidence, and did this in a thorough and conscientious fashion. After several assessment centres, some 'noise' began to be heard from very senior managers that this particular executive should not be allowed to continue to be an observer, because that person was biased. The bias was attributed to incidents in the past where the executive concerned had, for professional reasons, either advised individuals against certain actions or rebuked them after actions had been taken against professional advice, and things had gone wrong. It turned out to be impossible to convince people who had been observed by this executive that the assessment process was such that it minimized bias, and the executive was ultimately asked to leave the observer panel. The lesson here is that, if the only way of reducing attribution bias is to hire external observers, so be it, but it will inevitably add to the cost of assessment.

Finally, there is the cost of running the assessment centre itself. If it is run residentially, there are costs of travel and accommodation for observers and participants. Then there is the opportunity cost of attendance of the participants and observers (and, for the latter, a tangible cost if, for reasons suggested above, external observers are used). If role plays are used as exercises, it may be decided to use professional actors. It may also be decided to use an external source, say an experienced occupational psychologist, to supervise the evaluation of ratings by observers, prepare feedback reports and give individual feedback after the event. Add to this the cost of administration, and of the time required of the persons being assessed and their managers in post-assessment review, follow-up and monitoring, and a sizeable amount of money can be incurred. Clearly, therefore, assessment as a method of individual needs analysis must be used selectively. Going back to our definitions in Chapter 2, assessment should represent a long-term development investment in the individuals concerned, and that may mean that its use is restricted to those deemed to have above average potential.

Conclusions

The three methods of identifying individual management development needs examined above – appraisal, 360-degree feedback and assessment – are not the only ones. Others include needs which are surfaced during the routine of work, or from permanent role changes or temporary assignments, such as to a project or working party. A mentoring relationship should normally be expected to reveal development needs, and some ways of addressing them (Kram, 1986). Some types of development programme, too, may identify needs, particularly if they include diagnostic techniques such as the use of 360-degree feedback.

Sadly, it appears that despite all the opportunities for the formal use of feedback to identify what development might be useful to managers, they are not generally exploited. Nicholson and West (1988), based on a sample of over 2300 British managers, found that: 'Almost two thirds have never received any kind of formal appraisal of their performance ... Most feedback comes from directly task related sources: clients, customers, and contacts, or concrete job indicators' (p. 165). Note, too, their following findings about managers who had recently had a change of role:

> The results show that one source of learning is valued above all other – on-the-job experience – but again there is cause for concern about deficiencies in other areas. Of these recent job changers 40–50% find their bosses 'not very useful' in any of the three learning areas. Previous job holders or other

concurrent job holders are of negligible use ... Colleagues and subordinates seem to have more to teach our sample than their bosses, even on such concrete matters as standards and methods and, interestingly, it is in the much more abstract area of organizational politics and interpersonal relations that colleagues' help is especially rated.

(Nicholson and West, 1988: 170)

These researchers conclude that (pp. 171–2):

The results suggest that most organizations display an almost contemptuous neglect of the provision of formal aids to learning and adjustment. It looks very much as if in most organizations, thinking about managerial training does not go beyond the 'strategy' of throwing managers into the deep end to learn by themselves ... This may produce adequate, and, on occasions, even excellent performance, but it leaves much to chance, is unlikely to establish a climate of attentiveness to career needs, and does nothing to establish either loyalty or controlled adjustment to performance requirements.

More recently, Storey *et al.* (1997: 228), in a comparative study of Japanese and British organizations, tell a similar tale:

To the extent that there was a generic British approach, it lay in a 'sink or swim' attitude to career development, a reliance on specific performance targets, and a stress on the 'ownership' of the career by the individual who then had to find a way through the internal and external labour market, drawing where relevant on an organization's resources.

I opened this chapter by questioning whether it is possible to arrive at an analysis of management development needs which successfully integrates all relevant organizational, job and individual factors. The answer is that, while we are unlikely ever to achieve something resembling a total analysis, we have at our disposal some very useful techniques which allow us to go a good deal of the way. At the individual level, assessment appears to offer a particularly thorough and revealing method and, though expensive, most organizations would surely have to agree that their best prospects are worth it. But, as Nicholson and West, and others (see Chapter 3 above), have found, many organizations are not making that effort, possibly because they fear it is too difficult, but possibly – and this is a more sinister explanation – that it has never occurred to them that they should.

7

MANAGERS LEARNING:
SOME USEFUL THEORIES,
SOME QUESTIONABLE RHETORIC

In the last chapter we began to look at how managers learn, in the context of development centres. Recall our senior general manager and her need to become more competent in knowledge sharing and project evaluation, and what types of intervention might best meet the different types of learning needed for each of those competencies. These are pedagogic considerations, concerned with what strategies are most appropriate for particular learning tasks, and I shall explore and critique some of them here, with particular reference to managers.

A first, if perhaps obvious, point to make is that managers are adults. A second point is that, as we saw in Chapter 2, a vast amount of management development is offered in the form of short courses, and delivery of these usually takes place in classrooms which, apart from the quality of the furniture and equipment, and the availability of confectionery and fizzy water, are much like the settings in which the managers learned as children. Even so-called 'learning in the outdoors' could be seen as taking the lessons from the classroom out to the school playing field. Nearly 30 years ago Rogers (1971) made the following comments about adult learning:

In adult education, and to a lesser extent in industrial training, innumerable classes exist where the teacher does most of
the talking, whether this is by lecturing or demonstrating . . .
Some tutors who enjoy talking, and know they are good at it,
will say defensively that their classes often compliment them
on their lovely performances and that their personal
charisma is what draws students in. This may be so, but
whether it *keeps* students and whether, furthermore, it keeps
out more than it keeps in, and whether students are actually
learning, is another matter . . . Far too many lecturers and
demonstrators assume that their listeners have some hole in
the head into which information can conveniently be poured
. . . In general it would seem that 'activity learning' is much
more suitable, because once they have tried it most adults
greatly prefer it to the passive, polite, imitative stuff which
they have previously encountered.

(Rogers, 1971: 57–8)

Depressingly, the only thing which seems to have changed
since that was written is that nowadays we do not use the term
'industrial training' very much. The general perception of
management development is based on the model of the short
course, delivered in a classroom environment, where participants are kept awake and amused by the presenter's ability to
deliver material in an entertaining way. Admittedly, it is not all
delivered in the form of lectures; there is often something of an
'activity' element, but activity of little more depth than the average party game. Common management training course clichés
include 'ice-breaker' exercises, treasure hunts, building models
from toy bricks, cutting out and pasting magazine pictures, and
even dressing up. Rogers's comment above on 'lovely performances' is an astute one. In this world of learning *qua* entertainment, it is presumed that the 'audience' wants to see a good
performance, and that it will be disappointed if it does not go
away feeling as though it has experienced an uplifting 'show'.
This phenomenon seems to be a naturally occurring one, even at
very senior levels of management. Witness the existence of
the guru circuit, those consultants and academics who earn
very large amounts of money by performing in front of senior

management audiences. As Clark and Salaman (1996: 92) have observed:

> . . . a key aspect of successful performances given by management gurus is the successful management of risk, promise and opportunity within a particularly highly demanding type of public performance, that carries a risk of total public failure and acclaim . . . the successful ones use their ability to manage this performance risk to build their personal 'characters' or reputations with clients.

It is a matter of concern that such performances should be perceived as vehicles for 'learning'. Perhaps, like the author, those readers who have attended such a performance have heard members of the audience say something afterwards like 'I really got a lot out of that.' The question is rarely asked: '*What*, exactly, did you get?' New, usable knowledge? Or was it reinforcement of your existing prejudices? Or just escapism?

I make two observations about such performances, based on my own experience. First, it is remarkable how many performers seem to work from the same script. Like jokes among club comedians, the same anecdotes get round gurus very quickly. Readers who are familiar with information technology and have long memories might recall that, in the early 1980s, when the clarion cry was 'information for competitive advantage', the name of American Hospital Supply was on every consultant's lips. (It was amazing how many of them claimed to have been personally and directly involved in that particular project.) When re-engineering began to achieve prominence, Proctor and Gamble became a fund of war stories. If the topic were leadership in the early 1990s, tales of Jack Welch at General Electric or of Lee Iacocca at Chrysler began to loom large.

The second interesting feature of gurus is how rarely they deviate from their scripts. It is possible to hear a guru address one management audience, and a completely different one some time later, and find that the scripts are almost exactly the same. It raises the interesting possibility that, when senior managers secure the services of such speakers, they are seeking to buy something safe and familiar, rather than have their preconceptions challenged. Much of what passes for 'management development', when it is from the mouths of gurus and their proselytes, represents a fascinating and eminently researchable phenomenon (Bloomfield and Vurdubakis, 1996), but the amount of learning which actually takes place at such events must be open to question.

How people – and, in the context of this book, how managers – learn is as important as *what* they learn. It follows from the approach we have taken so far that as we move from identifying organizational through job to individual needs, we hopefully build an increasingly accurate picture of what needs to be learned. At this point, thought should be given to how it could be, and ultimately will be, learned. This will lead to conclusions about the choice of learning method. The management developer should strenuously resist the temptation to move from ideas about needs to ideas about programmed instruction. It is just too easy to take the path from needs to learning objectives to course design or selection, and this could well result in an inappropriate intervention for the individual manager whose needs we are trying to address. A more fruitful approach is to consider what learning theory or theories might usefully inform our decision on how learning is most likely to be accomplished in a given case. Noe *et al.* (1997: 179) identify five 'useful theoretical frameworks for studying development activities': social learning theory, expectancy theory, goal setting theory, theory of reasoned action and contract theory. Let us examine each of these to see what each could specifically bring to decisions about management development.

Social learning theory

This was developed by Bandura (1977a), and described by Latham and Saari (1979: 239–40) thus:

> Social learning theory explains human behaviour in terms of a continuous reciprocal interaction among cognitive, behavioural and environmental determinants ... Social learning theory specifically acknowledges that human thought, affect, and behaviour are influenced by observation as well as by direct experience. It states that people use symbols to create, to communicate, to analyse conscious experience, and to

engage in foresightful action. Moreover, the theory states that people do not merely react to external influences but actually select, organize and transform stimuli that impinge on them.

One particularly interesting aspect of social learning theory is concerned with self-efficacy (Bandura, 1977b), and the notion that individuals can develop their competence at tasks vicariously, by observing and modelling the behaviour of others. As Bandura (1977b: 192) puts it:

Because acquisition of response information is a major aspect of learning, much human behaviour is developed through modelling. From observing others, we form a conception of how new behaviour patterns are performed, and on later occasions the symbolic construction serves as a guide for action . . .

In contrast, the attempted use of persuasion to convince people that they can cope better with particular situations is less successful:

Efficacy expectations induced in this manner are also likely to be weaker than those arising from one's own accomplishments because they do not provide an authentic experiential base for them . . . Simply informing participants that they will or will not benefit from treatment does not mean that they necessarily believe what they are told, especially when it contradicts their other personal experiences.

(Bandura, 1977b: 198)

An important implication of this is that one of the most potent sources of management learning is the behaviour of people whom managers see as significant and successful. It would be a fair guess that such people are the very senior managers in the organization. I would therefore argue that senior management behaviour holds more capacity for raising (or not) individual management competency than most, if not all, other forms of intervention – training courses, assignments, mentoring, coaching and everything else in the management developer's trick-bag. It is therefore somewhat ironic that it is often a factor which management developers find difficult to change. In Chapter 2 I drew attention to Argyris's

(1990: 23) distinction between managers' espoused theories and their theories-in-use, and the differences we often see between what managers say *should* be done and what they actually do. If we follow Bandura's thinking about learning being more effective when it has an authentic experiential base, then what is it that subordinates will really learn from managers?

Take, as an example, the case of 'performance management'. Senior managers might well cite this as 'a good thing' and one worth implementing throughout the organization in the interests of productivity, improved cash flow or some other criterion of organizational effectiveness. The top team decides, on the strength of a convincing presentation by management consultants, that goal setting and appraisal will be implemented top-down throughout all levels of management. It further decides that the main method of effecting this change will be through standardized training, where all managers will learn to change their behaviour from their current largely informal style to one of rigorous objective setting, quarterly individual appraisals, new forms, a computer-based monitoring system and a supporting bureaucracy.

The training begins. The members of the top team have their training, with much noise, symbolism and coverage in the company newsletter. As the training programme works its way down the hierarchy the level of noise diminishes, but nevertheless a 'common message' is being carried downwards. Many managers become very enthused about it, expressing their enthusiasm in terms such as: 'It's great because at last we seem to be speaking a common language.' But just as the training is beginning to gain a foothold in middle management and first-line supervisory circles, the word leaks out that a number of the top team members, including the chief executive, have not yet got round to setting objectives for those who report directly to them. Reasons are offered why this is so: 'There was a crisis with a very large client who threatened to stop doing business with us'; 'Our subsidiary in Australia needed a lot of top management attention'; 'There was an important and delicate merger deal with a company in the Far East.' Many managers feel let down, others feel relieved. In both cases, the motivation to apply the performance training palpably diminishes among the management population.

This vignette, though imaginary, will probably be familiar to seasoned management developers. Lest we all succumb to depression about the negative implications of social learning theory, let us turn to a case which nobly demonstrates its positive application to managerial learning. Latham and Saari's (1979) study is a classic one, on at least two counts. First, it shows how, through an imaginative research design, psychology theory can be successfully applied, in an undiluted and authentic way, to management performance problems. Those who consider themselves too pragmatic to bother their heads with 'academic' sources of business solutions should take heed. Second, it applies longitudinal evaluation measures of its effects on trainee performance based on data collected about trainee reactions, learning achievement and behavioural change (Kirkpatrick, 1959), an important point to which I shall return in the next chapter. The problem which Latham and Saari set out to address was to improve the performance of 100 first-line male managers in a US-based international company, in terms of nine specific outcomes, including motivating poor performers, reducing absenteeism and overcoming resistance to change. For the first 40 managers to receive training, they assigned 20 to a training group and 20 to a control group, but – and here is a clever touch – 'the people assigned to these two groups did not know that they had been labelled as a control or an experimental group. They assumed that for logistical reasons, they were among the first or last to receive the training' (Latham and Saari, 1979: 241).

The training itself took place during weekly two-hour sessions over nine weeks (not, note, in a two-day cram at a conference centre). The managers were shown films depicting a 'model' manager effectively handling a situation concerned with the business objectives of the exercise, e.g., motivating a poor performer, at the end of which learning points were shown. The managers then discussed the performance of the 'model', and took part in one-on-one, unscripted role playing of a similar but real situation in which they had recently been involved, observed by the other participants. Finally, participants were asked to give feedback to the role player on the effectiveness of his behaviour in that situation. At the end of the nine-week period, the managers were instructed to apply what they had learned to their jobs within the following week, and to report their successes and failures to the learning group afterwards. Interestingly, at an early point in the process – which was mandatory for the participants – there was some antagonism shown: 'The lack of receptiveness was evident at the initial training classes when the supervisors stared at the floor with observable frowns' (p. 242). By the third session, however, the managers had begun to warm to the process. Latham and Saari recorded this participant's comment (p. 242):

> Most training isn't worth ____; it works in the classroom, but not on the job. With this program, it is just the opposite. It is much easier to do on the job what we learned here than it is to do it in front of all of you.

At the end of the training for the first group of 20, their job performance, based on their superintendents' ratings and the organization's traditional appraisal instrument, was significantly better than that of the control group. Crucially, the job performances of training group and control group members had been rated before the training, and no significant difference had been found. Moreover, once the control group had received their training one year after the experimental group, there was found to be no significant difference between their subsequent performance levels and those of members of the experimental group; the training had 'worked' equally well for them. Latham and Saari concluded that:

> The theoretical significance of this research is that it demonstrates that the integration of both cognitive and behaviouristic principles within the context of social-learning theory brings about a relatively permanent change in supervisory behaviour in what to supervisors is the most difficult part of their job, *managing people.*
>
> (Latham and Saari, 1979: 245, emphasis added)

Latham (1989) has since, citing Burke and Day (1986), recorded that 'a meta-analysis of seventy studies on the effectiveness of management training showed that behaviour modelling is among the most effective training methods' (p. 271). It must remain a mystery why, despite such compelling evidence, so much training and development activity supposedly aimed at improving the way managers manage people continues to be done in classroom settings, with non-authentic methods and apparatus.

Expectancy theory

This is one of several *instrumentality* theories of motivation (Landy, 1989: 379), so called because they seek to answer the question of how people view performing a particular action, or set of actions, as being instrumental to their achieving a particular outcome. Take an example of dealing with a broken television set, where the desired outcome is a working television set. One individual might rate her ability to mend television sets as high, and therefore that her own work on the broken set will be instrumental to its repair. Another individual might see taking the set to a professional television repairer as instrumental, yet another that purchase of a new set would be instrumental, and so on. Vroom (1964) offers a particular version of this theory – valence, instrumentality and expectancy (VIE) theory. Valence is the value which the individual places on the outcome – how much do I value a working TV set? Instrumentality is the belief the individual holds that a given action will lead to a given outcome – what could I do to obtain a working TV set? Expectancy is the individual's subjective judgement of the probability of a given action's success – what are the chances of ending up with a working TV set if I, say, try to mend it myself? Vroom holds that the relationship between these three variables as to their effects in motivating an individual to exert effort is multiplicative: Effort = Σ (Valence $\times$ Instrumentality $\times$ Expectancy). It follows from this logic that if any of the three variables is absent in a given situation, no effort will be expended.

This theory has been with us for a relatively long time, so it is not surprising that it has been tested through research, and comprehensively questioned (see Landy, 1989: 385–9). However, it does offer an interesting model of motivation as a process, particularly when it is applied to how managers relate their learning to success, be it organizational, personal or both. It raises, for example, the question of how managers view management education. Do they see education specifically in management as something of value? According to Grey and French (1996: 3–4), the response to that question is equivocal:

> ... there is no occupational closure around practising as a manager; it is quite legal, and commonplace, to be a manager without receiving any training or accreditation. Nevertheless, it could be argued that increasingly management is becoming *de facto* if not *de jure* a professionalised activity, especially through such initiatives as the MBA qualification, the development of the British Academy of Management, the Management Charter Initiative in the UK, or the American Assembly of Collegiate Schools of Business in the United States. Plainly, however, this process is not very far advanced, at least within the UK ... Second, it is by no means clear that a trained manager is more effective than an untrained one, whereas it is generally accepted that a trained doctor is more effective than an untrained one.

This clearly goes back to the 'elusive phenomenon of management' issue which I raised in Chapter 2. The valence of a degree in medicine to practising as a doctor is so obvious, both to the medical profession and to the public at large, that it can go virtually unquestioned. From the instrumentality perspective, the only way of obtaining a degree in medicine is through an accredited course at a university, and one's Advanced Level examination results and the university's selection, continuous assessment and examination procedures are the major sources of expectancy about a successful outcome.

But management is different. How might an 18-year-old who is interested in a career in management make a judgement between pursuing a university degree in, say, business studies and trying to find an employer willing to recruit her into a young managers' training scheme? What, ultimately, will be more greatly valued by future employers? The instrumentality for both options could be exactly the same (that is, a reasonable set of examination results), although the expectancy will be subject to other factors, like the availability of university places for relevant degree courses or of management training schemes for 18-year-olds. This type of dilemma will probably occur again and again throughout a manager's career. Should she, under pressure from her boss, attend that two-week sales training programme, even though she can see no prospect of ever performing a sales role? She might recognize that there is no intrinsic short-term value in so doing, but that in the organization where she works (the one, perhaps, which experienced the performance management training failure I described in the last section), most of the top people have a sales background, and they see the sales training course as a rite of passage for anyone seeking advancement.

For the management developer trying to help an individual manager with choices about development, expectancy theory can be useful. Let us suppose that, following attendance at an assessment centre, a manager has displayed a low level of competency in strategic planning. During subsequent discussions with his boss and the management developer, a number of actions are agreed: that the boss more actively involves him in the planning process for the division; that she gives him coaching in how she handles the process; that he spends the next three months developing a two-year plan for his own department, using what he learns from his boss as guidance; and that he attends a formal, three-week programme on business strategy at a high-profile international business school to obtain specific knowledge about analytical models and best practices. A month after this agreement is obtained the developer follows it up, and discovers that the actions are being implemented, other than the business school programme, which has not yet been arranged. The manager states that he would greatly value the programme (positive valence) and expects it to be of great practical value (positive instrumentality), but that he has a very busy period ahead and is unlikely to find the time to attend the programme in the next 12 months (negative expectancy).

Based on this information, the developer decides to explore some possibilities with the manager and his boss, such as rescheduling priorities, allowing slippage in certain projects in which the manager is involved and ensuring that key aspects of his work are adequately covered while he is attending the business school programme. It is easy to argue that one does not need to know expectancy theory in order to come to such conclusions and recommendations. The counter-argument to this is possibly yes, but in the absence of a theoretical framework, would an explanation for the manager's behaviour have been sought in the first place?

Goal setting theory

This is another theory of individual motivation which, claims Latham (1989: 272), 'is among the most scientifically valid and useful motivational theories in organizational science'. The essence of the theory, which owes a great deal to the experimental work of Locke (1968, 1970), is described by Landy (1989) thus:

> (Locke's) major proposition is that harder goals yield higher performance (but only if the individual *accepts* these goals). He has shown consistently that individuals who set or accept harder goals perform at levels higher than those who set or accept easier goals.
>
> (Landy, 1989: 402, original emphasis)

Again, this theory has been around long enough to be tested and critically reviewed by other researchers (see Landy, 1989: 404–6), but it continues to be cited frequently, particularly in the context of performance management (Williams, 1998). Latham (1989: 272–3) has written of its application to individual develop-ment, particularly through *self-managed learning*:

> In brief, the training teaches people to assess problems, set specific hard goals in relation to those problems, monitor ways in which the environment facilitates or hinders goal attainment, and administer reinforcers for working toward (and punishers for failing to work toward) goal attainment.

Based on Latham's description, this approach is arguably as much about evaluation of learning as it is about the learning itself: '. . . training in self-management should improve transfer of train-ing to the job' (p. 284). My response to this proposition is yes, but . . . As I suggested in my comments on social learning theory, it will be more difficult to sustain one's programme of learning if the surrounding organizational environment does not reinforce it. It is not difficult to imagine how a passing comment from one's boss or peers might attenuate one's motivation to learn – 'You

91

should know by now, qualifications count for nothing round here'; 'If you paid as much attention to the real office politics as you did to that training course you went on, you might achieve something.' Nonetheless, goal setting theory offers another useful tool to management developers, as the following example shows.

In an executive development programme, each participant is asked first to consider, then to describe to other participants, a significant problem which will require a decision from him or her in the relatively near future. Over the course of the programme, participants are exposed, through case studies and other materials, to various business decisions, and asked to note which aspects of these are relevant to their own problems. They also work with one another in small groups to understand (and often reframe) their problems and develop tentative solutions. Towards the end of the programme, they are encouraged to develop an action plan, stating some explicit goals for how they are going to implement their decisions. As they do so, they are counselled to consider what factors in the workplace might facilitate implementation, and what might work against it, and how they intend to overcome obstacles. Since participants are usually widely dispersed around the world, and in senior positions in the organization, they know that they are 'on their own' once they are back at work, though occasionally they maintain contacts with individuals whose help they have valued during the programme. However, a fairly common occurrence which I observe, with some concern, is that participants do not always see their immediate bosses as particularly helpful counsellors, and have often not shared their problems with their bosses before attending the programme. Moreover, they frequently do not see bosses as sources of positive reinforcement for them through the difficult decisions they are having to make and implement. In these circumstances, self-managed goals might offer some help to the individual's learning, but are in danger of being lost, quite literally in the 'noise' of organizational activity.

Theory of reasoned action

This theory, which emanates from the experimental work of Ajzen and Fishbein (e.g., 1980),

... proposes that behaviour is determined directly by one's intention to perform the behaviour, and intention, in turn, is influenced by attitudes (i.e., one's positive or negative evaluations of performing the behaviour) and by subjective norms (i.e., the perceived social pressure to perform or not to perform the behaviour).

(Bagozzi and Kimmel, 1995: 439)

Although this theory and its derivative, the theory of planned behaviour (Ajzen, 1991), have been, and continue to be, major influences on the work of attitude theorists, I have rarely seen them cited outside the field of social psychology. Again, the theory's limitations have been amply considered (see, e.g., Jaspars, 1990: 274). However, the observant reader will have noticed that certain aspects of this theory resonate with aspects of the theories we have already examined. Let us try applying it to a management development situation.

Suppose that a manager has just completed an appraisal and has agreed with her manager that she would benefit from increasing her knowledge of business finance, particularly to help prepare her for the senior general management role to which she aspires. She agrees to attend an in-company 'Finance for Managers' course which is run on a regular basis. Many of her peers have already attended this course, and she knows they have rated it as very useful, so she schedules her attendance. Just before the programme is due to run, she withdraws from it, claiming pressure of work. This sequence of events is repeated, and the manager's boss asks the management development manager for advice.

The management development manager meets the manager concerned, and confirms that she does intend to attend this course, 'when I get the chance'. He concludes that the intention is genuine, and that the manager recognizes its beneficial consequences for her current job performance and her future career. The manager also acknowledges the social pressure – both from her boss and the organization at large – for her to attend this programme, and that it is the norm in this organization for someone of her level and experience to attend it. The management development manager wonders whether this manager may hold an attitude which is in some way holding her back from attending the course, even in the face of social pressure to attend it. From asking some questions, he elicits the belief by the manager that any learning she has found worthwhile she has 'learned by doing' rather than 'being taught by someone else'. She also claims that she has taken a test which has confirmed this.[1]

The management development manager concludes that the manager would, if she were forced, attend the course, but that because of a negative evaluation of theory-based learning, probably based on a long-established attitude, she might well resent it. Indeed, forcing her to comply is not likely to change her attitude towards this type of learning (Brown, 1985: 83) and could make the experience of the course so aversive for her that she actually learns very little (Mager, 1968: 49–60). What to do now? The developer feels that, in the long term, it would be in the manager's interests if her attitude towards theoretical learning were more positive, because there is likely to be a greater requirement for it at the senior management level to which she aspires. In the short term, however, she requires knowledge of how to interpret a profit and loss account, appreciate the time value of money, understand the principles of financial planning and control, make investment decisions and so on, to do her current job effectively. He decides that a gradual approach is called for, and recommends the following programme:

1 The manager will spend one day per week over the next 12 weeks with the finance department. On each of those days, she will observe, and work with, finance officers performing various functions such as budgeting and financial forecasting. The sequence of assignments will follow the sequence of contents in the set textbook for the 'Finance for Managers' course.
2 The manager will commit to reading the textbook over the 12-week period, but does not have to read each part until *after* she has had the experience of how the finance department performs that aspect of work in practice.
3 At the end of the 12-week period, the manager will attend the 'Finance for Managers' course, but will have the objective of evaluating its contents against what she has learned in the finance department. She will then discuss how closely the 'theory' of the course matches the 'practice' of the finance

department's work with the management development manager and the chief accountant.

The 'hardened realists' of the management development world might dismiss the above approach as too luxurious. If the manager concerned found it difficult to find the time just to attend the course, how could she possibly find time for 12 days' on-the-job learning *and* the course? Surely she should just be told to attend the course in the first place, and have done with it? This stance, which again tends to reflect a deep-seated attitude toward the nature of learning, is one which I have found quite common among managers and, sadly, among some management developers. It comes as a surprise to such people that managers like the one in our story above can attend training course after training course and still not 'learn' to perform as 'required', the blame being placed on the trainees rather than on the lack of imagination of their sponsors. Mager's (1968: 11) simple piece of advice should be heeded:

> One objective toward which to strive is that of having the student leave your influence with as *favourable* an attitude toward your subject as possible. In this way you will help to maximise the possibility that he (*sic*) will *remember* what he has been taught, and will willingly *learn more* about what he has been taught (original emphasis).

One further point should be made. As a way of diagnosing what could be termed the 'management learning difficulties' in the above case, the theory of reasoned action would not only have the advantage of a strong theoretical background and empirical support, but it would also be hugely *practical*, mainly because it seeks to explain behaviour. The same cannot be said for the ever-popular style-based approach, for exactly the same reasons, but negated: it doesn't have a strong theoretical background, is not well supported empirically and makes little attempt to explain behaviour beyond categorizing people according to their preferences.

Contract theory

Although the idea of the *psychological contract* can be traced back to the writing of Argyris (1970), it has recently been the subject of attention of other researchers, notably Rousseau (1995). Ratnasingam *et al.* (1998: 183) describe the concept thus:

> The psychological contract is defined as a set of beliefs held by a person regarding the terms of an exchange agreement to which the person is party . . . Thus psychological concepts are perceptual, reflecting beliefs about obligation that both parties have of each other, and beliefs about the extent to which those obligations have been fulfilled.

Whether or not this concept of the psychological contract deserves to be called a 'theory' is debatable (see the final section of this chapter), but it has without question started to become influential in Human Resource Management circles, and it has provided a platform for research, particularly since it is concerned with concepts about societal, as well as organizational norms (Herriot and Pemberton, 1995). By way of illustration, let us consider a typical, City-based UK financial services company in the 1970s. The 'feel' of such an organization at that time would typically be paternalistic, and the unwritten 'deal' – or psychological contract – between the employer and employees founded on loyalty. The employee was expected to show diligence, respect for senior personages and absolute trust in their decisions. The senior directors, for their part, offered long-term security, concern and welfare for employees and members of their families, and a relatively comfortable working environment.

Things began to change in the early 1980s, partly as a result of harsher economic and competitive conditions, but also through the emergence of a political and social climate strongly influenced by social Darwinism. Gradually, the idea that lame ducks should be carried along or nursed back to health by a caring, welfare-minded management regime began to give way to the idea that the kindest thing to do to lame ducks was to shoot them. There is evidence that this cultural outlook had gained considerable adherence in UK organizations by the 1990s (Evans *et al.*, 1992; Coopey, 1995).

One aspect of this climatic change in management development circles has been an increasing fashion for 'self-development', where the manager, rather than the organization, is expected to take the primary responsibility for his or her future development, though the organization is expected to 'facilitate' this learning in some way, for example by paying for attendance at formal programmes. A study of more than 500 UK managers (Handy *et al.*, 1996) showed that 'personal development plans' were the single largest source of development, and cited by 65 per cent of respondents as being available to them. Depending on one's outlook, this could be seen as either a healthy or unhealthy sign for management development. Roberts (1994: 15), for example, takes the view that it is essentially healthy because it is 'concerned with attainable realities – the difference between what the individual currently does and how and what s/he can realistically be expected to achieve', whereas many training courses take too passive an approach to learning. Coopey (1995: 67) takes a different view, arguing that self-development is an ideology through which the power system in organizations manifests its right to exercise control through individual accountability. In Coopey's view, self-development is not so much about individual 'improvement' so much as conformity to corporate norms.

It is possibly too early to assess the effects of the trend towards self-development for managers on managerial learning, and ultimately managerial performance. However, it should be possible to predict, from the other theories we have examined, in what conditions such an approach would be successful. For example, what outcomes would social learning theory and the theory of reasoned action predict for an organization where senior managers publicly espouse self-development, but show no signs of adopting such self-development themselves? What outcome would expectancy theory predict for an organization where managers believe they are perfectly capable of undertaking self-development, but do not associate it with things they value, such as a rate of promotion or salary increase which are greater than for those who do not undertake self-development? And what would goal setting theory predict as the outcomes for the organization which sets up a 'corporate university' with a faculty and courses, and then sends out the message that it is indifferent to a manager's *choice* of learning, as long as the manager demonstrates that *something* has been learned; that any 'growth' is valid? The words of Mueller (1996: 765) should be heeded:

The reaction to increased accountability is often the super-stitious institutionally motivated imitation of practices *as if* it was based upon solid knowledge. Indeed, empirical evidence regarding the 'rationality' of diffusion of supposedly best practice between firms is clouded by management's occasional or perhaps widespread desire to follow fashion (original emphasis).

Questionable rhetoric

It would not seem right to leave the subject of learning without some reference to the concept of 'the learning organization' (Senge, 1990). Since the publication of Senge's best-seller, *The Fifth Discipline* (1990), 'the learning organization' has become a very fashionable term in managerial and organizational development circles, often held up as a desirable objective and much cited in company mission statements. So pervasive has the idea become, especially in the field of Human Resource Management, that even writers of a critical persuasion and reputation seem reluctant not to pay homage to it (Mabey *et al.*, 1998: 310). It is almost too nice an idea to disparage. As Senge says (1990: 4): 'Learning organizations are possible because, deep down, we are all learners . . . Learning organizations are possible because not only is it in our nature to learn but we love to learn.' Senge's *The Fifth Discipline* is an engaging book, full of home-spun aphorisms ('The easy way out usually leads back in' [p. 60]; 'Dividing an elephant in half does not produce two small elephants' [p. 66]), imaginative, whimsical illustrations and anecdotes from contemporary life in US corporations. It also seems to dwell, as does most of the writing about learning organizations, in the realm of philosophical or metaphysical discourse (Popper, 1991: 197). Pedler *et al.* (1991: 3), for example, define a learning organization as 'an organization which facilitates the learning of all its members and continuously transforms itself'. As I mentioned in Chapter 4, this looks as if it is taking the metaphor of organization as organism just too far, to the point where the organization is not *like* an organism, but *is* an organism (Morgan, 1997: 69–71).

How, for instance, would one test for the presence of a learning organization, or effectiveness of such an organization compared to, say, an *un*learning organization? As Kelly (1963: 18) says:

> A theory may be considered as a way of binding together a multitude of facts so one may comprehend them all at once. When the theory enables us to make reasonably precise predictions, one may call it scientific. If its predictions are so elastic that a wide variety of conceivable events can be construed as corroborative, the theory fails to meet the highest standards of science.

Perhaps the only aspect of organizational behaviour which we can confidently predict will be influenced by the learning organization concept is that many senior managers will, for a while to come, spend large amounts of money trying to turn their organizations into learning ones. The learning organization is an attractive idea, and one which follows in the humanist tradition of organizational writing (Vroom and Deci, 1979). But I leave the final words on this subject to Mackenzie Davey and Guest (1996: 239):

> The learning organization is presented as a vague abstraction with no clear basis in theory or practice. There are those who argue in favour of such vagueness on a number of grounds. One is that there is more to life than can be understood by mere rationality; another argument is that since everything is changing all the time it is impossible to predict how things will be in future. Linked to this is the argument that as change transforms understanding it is not possible to anticipate the next steps. The response to these arguments may be to say why bother, or to point out, as Bob Mager does, that 'if you don't know where you are heading, you may end up some place else'.

Note

1 The 'test' to which the manager is referring is probably the *Learning Styles Questionnaire* (Honey and Mumford, 1995). This is based on Kolb's (1984) model of learning which posits a so-called 'learning cycle', a process whereby individuals seek concrete experience (*activist*

mode), apply self-observation and reflection to the data obtained (*reflector* mode), test the learning against abstract concepts and generalizations (*theorist* mode) and finally apply the learning in new situations (*pragmatist* mode). The *Learning Styles Questionnaire* seeks to identify whether respondents prefer to adopt one or more of these modes, or 'styles', when learning.

8

SELECTING, DESIGNING AND EVALUATING MANAGEMENT DEVELOPMENT INTERVENTIONS

I have purposely linked the actions of selection and design with evaluation for the simple reason that I think they are inseparable, though there is evidence that in practice they are often not considered that way. Thomson (1998: 6), citing a 1994 Industrial Society survey of 457 UK companies, notes that 19 per cent of them 'did not carry out any systematic evaluation beyond the end-of-course "happy sheet" stage'. The reasons for not doing so included difficulty in establishing measurable results, lack of time, lack of management support and lack of knowledge of evaluation techniques. I would be surprised, though very pleased, if the other 81 per cent of respondents to the Industrial Society survey were all carrying out systematic evaluation of their training in general, and management development in particular, but I fear this is unlikely. One reason is that, while few would claim that any training evaluation is easy, the evaluation of management training appears to be particularly difficult, not least because of a problem we have repeatedly encountered throughout this book. If it is difficult to pin down what managers do, or should do, it follows that it is difficult to specify how any training, education or development will help them to do 'it' better (Landy, 1989: 353). Yet it would be ironic if so much money should be poured into management training programmes without any systematic means of evaluating their worth. If it were really considered an 'investment', then surely senior managers, aided and abetted by their finance staff, would be looking for a 'payback'? While there is evidence that some do, and that there is a growing trend in that direction (Rainbird, 1994), clearly many do not (Tannenbaum and Yukl, 1992: 423).

I do not intend here to give extensive treatment to the principles and techniques of evaluation, which are well covered by other texts (see, for example, Patton, 1986; Bramley, 1992; Robson, 1993: 170–86). My main point, however, is that management developers, at the point when they are considering how to meet an identified development need through selecting or designing some form of intervention, should consider how they will evaluate the effectiveness of that intervention. A useful first question in this process is: what does *effectiveness* mean in the context of this particular development situation? A second is: how could we tell if effectiveness, as defined, had changed after the intervention? The first question is so fundamental that one might be tempted to think that it is always asked, perhaps not on a formal basis every time, but nevertheless asked. But as we saw in Chapter 2, training and development are largely supply-driven. Every working day, many tons of unsolicited brochures – frequently reinforced by unsolicited telephone calls – are delivered to training departments throughout the UK, offering 'solutions' to hard-pressed management developers, and trying to take away from them the burden of facing up to difficult questions about effectiveness. Surely the effectiveness of the programmes on offer is self-evident? Often effectiveness is equated with popularity: 'Thousands of managers have now benefited from our approach to stress management, outdoor team development, project management . . .'. The brochures offer testimonials – 'The most useful course I have ever attended. I'd recommend it to anyone who really wants to drive up team performance' (*Customer Services Manager, Retail Group, Newbury*).

The process is one where the supplier attempts to persuade the training department, which in turn attempts to persuade managers in its organization, to subscribe to the programmes on offer. The main object of this behaviour seems not to be about learning, or performance, but about *selling*. Training and development are reduced to the level of a commodity. As for airlines, hotels, theatres and restaurants, the critical success factor is to operate at full capacity, to sell the maximum number of seats. Given this outlook, it is hardly surprising that evaluation usually goes no further than seeking responses to a set of stock questions . . . 'Please tell us, where 0 = dissatisfied and 5 = delighted, how much you enjoyed your flight/stay/play/meal/training course.' It was once made clear to me, shortly after joining a training department, that one of the things expected of the training director was to use personal influence with line managers to 'sell' unallocated or cancelled places at internal training courses. The logic was that, if the places remained empty, the course would run 'at a loss'. Courses were therefore regarded as successful if they were popular, if they had 'gone down well' and their participants had persuaded others to attend future events. Whether anything had been learned, or behaviour changed, or organizational results improved (Kirkpatrick, 1959) was either taken for granted or ignored. Effectiveness was therefore equated with take-up.

Now, there is a lot to be said for making training experiences pleasant and enjoyable for participants so as to encourage learning (Mager, 1968). Also, organizations are right to expect that their training and development departments should be run efficiently and therefore that, if courses are to be used, their take-up rate should be reasonable. But let us not be led into believing that, as management developers, our greatest contribution to organizational effectiveness lies in offering popular programmes which at least break even. Recall some of the Schmitt and Klimoski criteria of organizational effectiveness given in Chapter 4, which contained items such as organizational growth and survival, leadership, control and decision-making processes. The problem with items like these is that, if asked to 'prove' that management development had any positive effect on these processes, it would be very difficult to do so. One could, however, improve one's confidence about the effectiveness of any given intervention by applying a thought process about precisely what change is wanted and expected from the intervention, and how the change might be assessed. I take the view that the thought process required can be usefully conceived of as a *research design*, which is 'concerned with turning research questions into projects' (Robson,

1993: 38). How would this work? Essentially, it would follow this process:

1 *Frame some appropriate questions*

Depending on the type of problem, examples of such questions might be pitched at the organizational, group or individual level. How do we raise the general level of managerial decision-making ability in this organization? How could we make the management team in our production division more capable at dealing with interpersonal conflicts? What development does our most promising sales manager need to enable her to succeed to the job of sales director, which is coming vacant in two years' time? Note that these questions are not plucked out of the air. There is a problem underlying each one – that most or all of our general managers are not good at decision making; that our production management team are poor at dealing with conflict; that our sales manager does not yet have all the knowledge, skills and abilities she needs to take over the sales director's job. The questions are therefore based upon judgements, which are (hopefully) based upon some objective data, that a change is required in management effectiveness which will lead, in turn, to improved effectiveness for the organization, as reflected in its results. Now, imperfect though aspects of this process might appear to be, we can at least be assured that it is a process which 'starts at the right end'; that a problem is in search of a solution, rather than the other way round.

2 *Develop some working hypotheses*

There are two main values of hypotheses. First, they prompt us to offer plausible explanations – 'interim guesses' (Robson, 1993: 29) – about the problems we are trying to address. Equally importantly, they begin to provide the wherewithal to test the effect of whatever we decide to do to address the problems. If we predict that a certain outcome will occur as a result of a particular intervention, we can start to consider how we can detect and measure the magnitude of that outcome. We have already encountered hypothesis forming in our consideration of learning theories in the last chapter. Recall how the various theories were used as the bases for hypotheses about what developmental approach might serve various needs, such as overcoming an individual's inhibitions about a particular learning method.

3 Decide what data to collect, and how to collect it

Since the intention of development is to change something (or, far less likely, but at the very least, to maintain the *status quo*), then the change needs to be measured to test whether, and to what extent, it has occurred. That requires measuring some aspects of what we want to change before applying whatever 'treatment' we think will work, and taking further measures of those aspects during the application of the treatment, at the end and possibly at some time afterwards, to check whether the change we wanted has been sustained. This seems so obvious as to be almost unnecessary, but inattention to measurement is the rule rather than the exception. At best, there may be a half-hearted attempt to measure reaction to the intervention shortly after its completion, usually going little further than a superficial measure of affect such as: 'Do you feel good about having attended this course?' But even at this level of measurement, there is usually no serious attempt to gauge cause and effect. How often are 'happy sheets' issued *before* a course starts? This comes back to the consumer sales model which I noted earlier as underpinning much of training and development. If one is selling training programmes in the same way as others sell televisions, knitwear or sausages, then the most one wants is an expression of post-sales satisfaction that will suggest the possibility of repeat business, positive testimonials and increased consumption. If, however, one is guided by the notion of development as *investment* (see Chapter 3), then it would be inconceivable not to take pre- and post-treatment measures to check for the effects of what one has done.

The choice of measure is not without difficulties. Take one of the examples given in Point 1 above: the team of production managers who appear to be having difficulties in handling conflict. This will be based on some observation, or reports of observation, and may well be expressed anecdotally, for example: 'That machine shop is a hot-bed of trouble. There are two or three troublemakers who are constantly bickering with one another and disrupting the work. Fred [the manager] doesn't seem to have a clue about how to deal with them.'

'Our supervisors seem to be pretty hopeless at dealing with problems between themselves. There's a components supervisor who's always complaining to me about the quality control supervisor, and the other way round. Why can't they talk about the problems themselves? Why do they come running to me for the answer?'

'I just came back from a management team meeting. You could have cut the atmosphere with a knife. It was obvious they were all seething about the decision on cutbacks, but not one of them said anything.'

A number of possible hypotheses about these problems might be offered, including:

- The *climate* of the production division is, in some sense, 'unhealthy', perhaps because of its relationships with other parts of the organization, or because the whole organization has been experiencing difficulties.
- The *competencies* of managers in the production division are low with respect to the ways they interact with each other and with their subordinates; they do not seem to hold people accountable.
- The problem rests with the production director, whose failure to clarify roles and responsibilities has led to confusion and uncertainty, and ultimately to unrest among the management team.

No doubt other possible explanations could be offered but, taking the three above, how would we attempt to operationalize the problem in such a way that would allow us to 'measure' it? If, for example, 'climate' is deemed the most plausible explanation, how could we attempt to collect data which represent the state of the current climate, and which could be collected again in future to see if any change had occurred? Likewise, if interpersonal competence is the general issue, how could we establish current and future levels of it? (Note that this task might well be facilitated if the organization has already established a model of managerial competencies, and methods for assessing individual levels of competency – see Chapter 5.) Finally, if the problem rests with the production director, how might we measure the effects of his current behaviour, and the effects of a future behaviour, attained either by developing an 'improved' production director, or by recruiting his replacement? I shall leave these as questions, in the hope that some readers may be moved to treat them as an exercise.

4 Select and design an appropriate intervention

I have already considered this to a certain extent in my examination of how to establish organizational, job and individual needs, but let us consider it again now as part of a flow of decisions and actions emanating from the research design. Here again, we are faced with having to develop a hypothesis, based on the data accumulated so far, about (using a clinical analogy) what form of 'treatment' is most likely to be effective in moving our management 'patient(s)' from their current 'unhealthy' (uninformed, unpractised, ineffective) state to a 'healthier' one, however construed. The hypothesis will undoubtedly follow an 'if, then ...' logic, for example: 'If we improve managers' knowledge of the causes and consequences of poor supervision of critical processes, then we will reduce waste [the problem identified by observation and data collection, in this case] and thereby reduce costs, so as to increase profits [the criterion of organizational effectiveness, in this case]. The way we think we could best improve that knowledge is through a specially constructed training programme.' The logic might well then be applied to some form of cost: benefit equation in which the expected cost of training x number of managers is offset against expected savings of y, and a payback calculated. In this way, the utility of the training is estimated in advance of the intervention. Alternatively, or additionally, some criterion of benefit might be used to help determine the design of the intervention. For example, if there were a standard that 'all training must start to show a positive return on expenditure after two years', that might well shape the management development manager's thinking about what training method is most likely to achieve this. Classroom training is relatively expensive and if – as it appears in this case – the major issue is managers' knowledge of process, then there may be other methods of transferring that knowledge (for example through literature, aural or visual aids) and testing for the presence of the knowledge before and after the intervention is made.

Not all management development interventions will call for a straightforward transfer of knowledge, as described in the example above. Given the long-term nature of development, it is arguable that many interventions will be more complex, and require considerably more thought and ingenuity. But the *logic* will be exactly the same. There will be some *criterion* or criteria of effectiveness and some *predictor* of what intervention is most likely to meet that criterion. Is this really the way that most choices about management development are made? My own experience is not necessarily so. I have frequently encountered, among management development peers, a phenomenon which might be termed 'my favourite things'. This phenomenon has its own logic, which does, it is true, follow an 'if . . . then' process, but simplified so that no matter what the presenting problem is, what follows is a set-piece solution with which the practitioner is both very familiar and very comfortable. So if the problem appears to be about ineffective interpersonal behaviour in a group of people, the practitioner recognizes the solution as 'team-building' and transports the group to Dartmoor for a week to hang by ropes off rock faces together, so that they will realize how dependent they are on one another, share a deeply cathartic experience and thereafter significantly modify their behaviour to one another in the workplace.

Even worse, the logic can readily be reversed into 'then . . . if', so that things which the practitioner knows and loves start to seek out development problems which might provide the opportunity to apply them. I recall a management development centre where it had been deemed that participants should, among other things, complete a particular personality inventory. When I asked why, I was told that it was because one of the facilitators was licensed to use that particular test, and that he 'always found it very useful'. Further probing revealed that no particular account had been taken of what the test results might explain or predict for the participants as far as their current or future effectiveness as managers was concerned. In another instance I recall working with a development manager who kept a very small number of training suppliers' course guides on a shelf beside his desk. Whenever a training need was raised his first instinct, long before the need had been discussed sufficiently to resemble analysis, was to reach for the shelf and find a 'fit'. He seemed quite proud about how quickly he could do this, seeing this as his particular 'value-added' contribution. Yet another development manager had an even narrower range of tactics. Whenever the first hint of a management development need appeared he would telephone his favourite training supplier and ask him to design an appropriate training course. Since the training supplier in question had an extremely narrow repertoire, all the courses he designed turned out to be very similar in substance so that, no matter what the problem actually was, the course was pretty well always the same. In that case, the development manager saw his contribution as ever being in a position to offer anybody, any time, a course (in effect, the *same* course!) for anything. The world of management development is rife with such antics and, much as one might like to attribute them to the incompetence of the developers concerned, the pervasive supply-driven mentality I noted earlier probably deserves the greater blame.

5 Implement the design and measure the results

Much has been written about designing development interventions, and it is a weighty subject in its own right (see, e.g., Goldstein, 1986; Holding, 1991; Lintern, 1991). I shall not explore it and all its intricacies here, but shall issue some caveats:

- *Beware the transfer trap.* Holding (1991: 93) points out that '. . . transfer is an extremely widespread phenomenon, playing a part in almost every instance of learning'. Baldwin and Ford (1988: 63) state that: 'For transfer to have occurred, learned behaviour must be generalised to the job context and maintained over a period of time on the job.' They go on to note that, according to research findings, '. . . while American industries annually spend up to $100 billion on training and development, not more than 10 per cent of these expenditures actually result in transfer to the job . . .'. The problem for the management developer is to implement a design which actually achieves not only a transfer of learning, but a sustainable transfer, and does not follow the 90 per cent of American interventions down the waste-pipe of failure. This is – fairly obviously – a difficult thing to achieve, sometimes depressingly so. How often, at the heady end of a week-long programme, is the management developer tempted to wonder: 'How much of what I have covered will have been forgotten by the middle of next week?' Baldwin and Ford (1988) offer some very useful thinking here. For example, they draw attention to the principle of 'identical elements', which 'predicts that transfer will be maximised to the degree that there are identical stimulus and response elements in the training and transfer settings' (p. 86). They distinguish between 'physical fidelity' – the extent to which the physical conditions of the development intervention match those of the work environment – and 'psychological fidelity', '. . . the degree to which trainees attach similar *meanings* in the training and organizational context' (p. 87, emphasis added).

A problem often encountered in development programmes is how to slow managers down, to distract them from their telephones, faxes and electronic mail, long enough to provide time for reflection. While acknowledging the difficulty of attaining physical fidelity, however, we must question why certain developers see a particular virtue in seeking physical *in*fidelity, such as through the use of outdoor development experiences. For a team of supermarket managers whose normal environment is check-outs and delicatessen counters, groping around in a dark, muddy cave in Derbyshire, trying to find the 'hidden object' before the other team finds it is hardly an example of 'identical elements', either in a physical or psychological sense. But even if transfer were attained and sustained, why go to all that trouble in the first place? If one wishes to simulate life in a supermarket, or an office, or a factory, why not use a supermarket, office or factory to do it? The answer, one suspects, has little to do with transfer of learning, and substantially more to do with popular notions that management development experiences ought to be 'different', 'exciting' and 'fun', in which case it might make equal sense to send trainees on a package holiday to Disneyland.

• *Beware over-elaborate designs.* There are two aspects to this. First, one should be absolutely clear about the learning objectives of a given intervention and stick to them. Second, one should avoid the tendency to load up the intervention with 'nice-to-have' features which might detract from or, worse, confuse the learning which actually takes place. I recall a project management programme I co-designed. At the start of the design process, the objectives were few and explicit, were related specifically to knowledge of the project management process (conceptualized as a cycle of activity), and were based on some key ideas obtained from a small number of well-researched project management texts. As the design progressed, new objectives began to creep in, bringing a clutch of nice-to-have features with them. 'The project leader will usually be leading a team. Shouldn't we do something about team leadership?' 'You know, interviewing seems to be an important method of collecting data for projects. We should say something about that. In fact, an interviewing exercise wouldn't go amiss.' And so on, until what had started as a plain vanilla sponge had been transformed, apparently without effort, into a rich fruit cake. From the reactions we received to the programme, there was no doubt that most participants enjoyed tasting the rich fruit, and our decisions to include them were thereby reinforced. However, had we stuck to our brief, the programme could have easily been run in two days, rather than the three that it actually took, and thereby at a substantially lower cost to the organization.

I have already noted the perversity of certain developers to include what they already know rather than what is needed, and intervention design is just too good an opportunity for such people to do 'what they always do': to pull out that old ice-breaker that 'never fails', or that box of toy bricks, or that neat little inventory that tells managers what type of leaders they are.

- *Beware poor administration*. Recall that this part of the process is about *implementing* an intervention, which means applying it as well as designing it. Having gained agreement from the appropriate authority to the design itself, there remains the task of setting up the intervention for whomever we have in mind for it and, to use the term commonly used these days, 'deliver' the intervention in some way, and possibly more than once. One interesting aspect of this is that, whereas in certain fields, such as engineering or information systems, it is acceptable to develop a prototype as a testing device prior to going into full production, this facility is not normally extended to management developers. Because we are incurring the cost both of the intervention, and of the participation of the managers concerned, we are expected to 'get it right first time', as well as every time thereafter. This is not as unreasonable as it looks, particularly as many interventions, especially those aimed at meeting wholly individual needs, are one-off in nature. If we recommend an expensive month-long business strategy programme at a major American business school to a highly paid executive, we do not have a second chance; either it meets that individual's needs or it does not.

It is sad, but in my experience true, that when interventions fail they often do so not because they are conceptually flawed or poorly designed, but because they are badly administered. Equally sadly, it is the bad administration which is remembered by the participants and sponsoring executive, apparently above all else. One of the executives nominated to attend the programme had already attended it, and no one registered the fact. The joining instructions were sent out too late, or did not give adequate directions to the conference centre. The accommodation was cramped. There were not enough copies of the programme materials . . . and so on. The successful delivery of development interventions needs to be orchestrated with painstaking attention to detail, and the value of an experienced and alert administrator should be weighed in gold.

Finally, let us turn to measuring the results. As emphasized in Point 3 above, the decision about what is to be measured should have been taken long before the intervention is made, and some pre-intervention measures already taken. Without them, post-intervention measures are virtually worthless. However, questions may arise about *when* to take post-intervention measures. Since, as I have repeatedly stressed, management development is a long-term process, it may be that whatever results are expected do not manifest themselves until long after the intervention has taken place. The problem is that, by then, many other variables may have intervened in the lives of the manager(s) and the organization which may have diminished, amplified or neutralized the effects of the intervention so far as the measured results are concerned. Kirkpatrick (1959) suggested that training results should be measured on four dimensions of effect: trainee reaction, learning accomplishment, changes in trainee behaviour and organizational results. Written in that order, these four items appear to represent four points of a scale of elapsed time and measurement difficulty. We would expect it to take far longer for an intervention to affect organizational results than to affect a manager's feelings. We would also expect it to be far more difficult to untangle the effects of a development intervention on organizational results from the effects of other influences, such as changes in structure, or technology, or in the environment in which the organization is operating. Moreover, organizations are not places which lend themselves readily to elegant experimental designs; it is difficult enough trying to identify the independent variables, let alone to control them. How could one hold the effects of the actions of competitors, or customers, or suppliers, or other parts of one's organization 'constant' while one takes a measuring rod to changes in the effectiveness of senior executives and tries to find some association with a programme they attended two years ago? In the face of such difficulties, one might well be tempted to throw in the towel, or pursue evaluation through a more radical, nebulous, post-modern alternative to conventional measurement such as 'responsive constructivist evaluation' (Guba and Lincoln, 1989: 46). Let us return to a classic study and see how two researchers applied their considerable ingenuity to an intervention design to overcome some of these problems.

Latham and Saari (1979): a case in point

I referred to this case in the last chapter when examining how learning theories – in that case, social learning theory – could be used to shape our decisions about development needs. It also provides a wonderfully clear – but sadly rare – example of how to apply the principles of research design to a management development problem. To see how it does this, I shall use the five-step approach outlined above to analyse the case. To recapitulate briefly: Latham and Saari undertook to provide training to 100 first-line supervisors at an international company in the United States. The object of the training was to improve the managers' interpersonal skills in dealing with subordinates, and it covered nine development needs: 'orienting a new employee, giving recognition, motivating a poor performer, correcting poor work habits, discussing potential disciplinary action, reducing absenteeism, handling a complaining employee, reducing turnover and overcoming resistance to change' (p. 241). In today's terminology, such a programme would probably be called 'performance management'.

Step 1: Frame some appropriate questions

Latham and Saari do not explicitly state what their research questions were, though it is possible to draw some reasonable inferences about them from the text of their article. Clearly, one of the questions was 'how effectively can social learning theory be applied to the development of managers?' More specifically, they wanted to find out how a particular programme based on behavioural modelling, and developed by Sorcher (Goldstein and Sorcher, 1974), could be applied 'to increase the effectiveness of first-line supervisors in dealing with their employees' (p. 240). They also wanted to find out the extent to which application of social learning theory could bring about 'a relatively permanent change in supervisory behaviour in what to supervisors is the most difficult part of their job, managing people' (p. 245). Another question was how to improve on predominant methods of evaluation of management training programmes, which they describe thus:

> The typical approach to the evaluation of a training programme is to review the programme with one or two vice presidents, various managers in the field, and perhaps a group of prospective trainees. If the programme 'looks good', the company uses it until someone in a position of authority decides that the programme has outlived its purpose. All of this is done on the basis of opinion and judgement. In the end, no one really knows whether the training attained the objectives for which it was designed.
>
> (Latham and Saari, 1979: 245)

Some of these questions are, to be sure, not of the type which management developers are accustomed to ask in the normal organizational context. (One wonders how a request to a senior executive to go and apply social learning theory in his or her part of the organization might be received.) But the question of achieving a relatively permanent change in managers' behaviour in terms of the way they manage people is at the very heart of the management developer's job. We face this question day in, day out.

Step 2: Develop some working hypotheses

Again, Latham and Saari do not state these explicitly in their article, but it is possible to infer what they are from their descriptions of the procedure they used, and their results. It would appear that at least the following hypotheses were developed:

- That participant reactions to the training programme immediately after its completion and at a later time (eight months afterwards) would be positive and consistent.
- That learning about difficult supervisory situations, as measured by a test of knowledge, would be significantly stronger in the 20 supervisors in the 'experimental' group, after they had completed their training programme, than in the 20 in the 'control' group, who had not (at the point at which the experimental group completed their programme) begun theirs.
- That measures of behavioural effectiveness, as rated by independent expert judges, would be significantly higher for members of the experimental group after training than for the control group before training.
- That measures of job performance, as rated by the supervisors' managers and by the organization's appraisal instrument, would be significantly higher for members of the experimental group after training than for the control group before training.
- That after the control group had received exactly the same training as the experimental group, measures of their reactions, learning, behaviour changes and job performance would not be significantly different from those of the experimental group.

Step 3: Decide what data to collect, and how to collect it

Having formulated their hypotheses and established some measures, Latham and Saari then collected data relevant to each hypothesis. By deciding on an experimental design, where one group was to receive the training first and the other group afterwards (using, as I noted in the last chapter, the perfectly legitimate reason that it was more practical to conduct the training as two consecutive programmes of 20 participants each, than one group of 40), they ingeniously created the opportunity to measure the effects of their interventions in the experimental group while holding the control group 'constant'. Practitioners would be well advised to remember this device when introducing a new programme. As Latham and Saari put it: 'In a situation in which it is impossible to train everyone simultaneously, there is no reason not to use a control group' (p. 245). To attempt to overcome bias, the researchers selected 40 supervisors at random from the total population of 100, then assigned 20 at random to the training group and 20 to the control group. The supervisors did not know they had been categorized in this way, only that they were members of either the first group to receive training, or the second. The measurements made for each of the four criteria are summarized in Table 8.1.

It can be seen that the measures used by these researchers were well planned and extremely thorough. They were also, however, parsimonious; Latham and Saari did not succumb to the 'over-elaborate design trap' I mentioned earlier.

Table 8.1 Summary of data collected for the study

Criterion	Data collected	When collected
Reaction measures	Questionnaire containing five questions, each with a 5-point Likert-type scale	1. Immediately after the final training session 2. Eight months after training was completed
Learning measures	Each trainee completed a test containing 85 situational questions[1]	1. At the end of the experimental group's training period, for the experimental and the control groups 2. For the control group at the end of their training period

Table 8.1 Continued

Criterion	Data collected	When collected
Behavioural measures	Tape-recorded role plays of supervisors resolving supervisor–employee problems[2]	1. At the end of the experimental group's training period, for the experimental and control groups[3] 2. For the control group at the end of their training period
Job performance measures	1 Ratings against 35 behavioural items of each supervisor by his line manager ('superintendent')	1.1 One month before the experimental group's training period, for the experimental and control groups 1.2 One year after the training, for both groups
	2 Ratings using the company's performance appraisal tool, containing 12 behavioural items	As for 1.1 and 1.2 above

Notes

1 'The questions were developed from critical incidents obtained in the job analysis ... of supervisory behaviour' (p. 243). (See also Chapter 5 of this volume.) 'Prior to administering the test, superintendents behaviourally anchored 1 (poor), 3 (mediocre), and 5 (excellent) answers for each question so that the trainees' responses could be objectively scored from 85 to 425 points.'

2 The role plays were based on scripts developed for each of the nine training topics in the programme. They were evaluated by 15 superintendents, who worked in groups of three, and who were 'blind as to the identity of each supervisor and whether the supervisor had received training' (p. 244). Their ratings were then 'compared with those of a second set of judges, consisting of the two trainers and the personnel manager'.

3 Another neat trick here ... During the role play sessions, the 20 experimental group supervisors were give the appropriate set of learning points for use during the role play, but 'Of the 20 foremen in the control group, 10 were given the learning points to determine whether knowledge alone of what one is "supposed to do" is sufficient to elicit the desired behaviour'. (The findings showed that the two control sub-groups did not have significantly different ratings to one another, but that the ratings for members of the experimental group were consistent with one another, but significantly higher than for those of the two control sub-groups.)

Source: Latham and Saari (1979)

Step 4: Select and design an appropriate intervention and
Step 5: Implement the design and measure the results

These have largely been covered above, and in our reference to this study in the last chapter. However, there are two further points which are worth making. The first is that Latham and Saari, despite their rigorous attention to controlling for relevant variables and measuring for their effects, were prepared to improvise at times and deviate from their 'script' if they felt it would be helpful to their trainees. For example: 'In several instances the learning points developed by Sorcher were not rigidly followed. In situations in which there was group consensus among the trainees that a learning point from one session should be added to another session, the learning points were rewritten' (p. 241). One might surmise that one of the ways that Latham and Saari overcame the considerable initial resistance from the training group was by demonstrating flexibility.

The second point was the extent to which these researchers involved the surrounding organization in this project, not least the supervisors' line managers (called 'superintendents') who contributed to the design of the measures, but also had to be trained in rating behavioural and job performance measures to a high standard, in order to ensure high reliability of the ratings. All in all, this study was a masterpiece of design and execution, but the management development practitioner should not be overawed by it. We might not be able to come quite up to Latham's and Saari's standards every time, but with attention to the principles of design, a working knowledge of relevant theories, practice, patience and not a little courage, we should expect to come fairly close.

9

SOME ALTERNATIVE
PERSPECTIVES, SOME FINAL
REFLECTIONS

In this final chapter, I shall explore some different angles on management development before summarizing the key points of the book and finally reflecting on how we can most effectively manage management development in organizations. My approach here will be rather more speculative, and possibly more provocative, than it has been in previous chapters. My main question here is what people, and particularly managers, see the *ends* of management development to be. After all, management development cannot be, much as developers might like it to be, an end in itself. It must surely serve some purpose other than to have 'developed managers' in one's organization. Let me review a number of perspectives before coming to some conclusions about what management development is for.

Management development as the professionalization of management

In Chapter 2 I drew attention to 'the elusive phenomenon of management' and the problems this caused for management developers. An attempt, strongly influenced by the writing of Handy (1987) and others, was begun in the UK in the late 1980s to professionalize management through education. The main agent of this attempt was the Management Charter Initiative (MCI), a quango with representation from organizations, government agencies, the Institute of Management and some academic sources, which took on the heroic task of trying to create a universal job description for any and all managerial roles, past, present and future. By defining management work, and qualifying its efficacy in terms of *standards,* the intention was that the knowledge and understanding required to perform to these standards could be codified, operationalized, taught, assessed and ultimately accredited by way of vocational qualifications. And indeed, this has come to pass. There *are* MCI codified standards described as 'key roles, units of competence and their associated elements of competence' (Salaman, 1995: 43–4), and there are vocational qualifications at various levels which accredit knowledge and demonstration of these standards. The standards themselves are a taxonomist's dream, showing meticulous classification of tasks and sub-tasks. In organizations, and at institutions of further and higher education, students are striving to learn what it means to manage 'operations', 'finance', 'people' and 'information' to a standard which will earn them a certificate or diploma. Elsewhere, bodies known as 'Training and Enterprise Councils' (TECs) are contributing to management professionalism by promoting the Management Charter ideal, along with National Vocational Qualifications, the 'modern apprenticeship' and other interventions. There exists a veritable soviet of teachers, trainers, students, assessors, verifiers, examiners and consultants whose livelihood hangs on this idea. However, at the time of writing, the idea is beginning to look decidedly past its sell-by date. Its take-up is low in relative terms, and there is little evidence of research to examine its effects (which may simply mean that researchers are not very interested in it).

What has happened? In a prescient critique, Reed and Anthony (1992) identified serious flaws in the implementation of the Management Charter Initiative:

The underlying ideological tensions and contradictions between an enterprising or entrepreneurial value system on the one hand, and a professional or status and control-orientated strategy on the other, were hardly recognised, much less debated or resolved. The organizational problems and political conflicts likely to accrue from these underlying tensions were also left unresolved. For the most part, they were sublimated within a pragmatically-oriented drive to 'do something' about the parlous state of management education, development and training in the UK as quickly as possible, while ensuring that the initiatives taken were soaked in the rhetoric of the 'enterprise culture' and the ideological and political sensitivities it catered for within governing institutions.

(Reed and Anthony, 1992: 592)

Now, the Management Charter Initiative may have been less successful than hoped because of poor implementation; many – perhaps most – good ideas fail for the same reason. But was (is) it a good idea in the first place? There are two underlying questions here, the first of which is, 'What is the value of professionalizing management?' Would the existence of professional qualifications make managers who possessed them more effective than managers who did not possess them? This must remain a mystery unless or until somebody undertakes some substantial research into the performance of managers who have obtained MCI-based qualifications versus those who have not. The second question is more technical, and that is whether it is realistic to base management development on job analysis which has been attempted at a level – in the MCI case at a national level – higher than that of a single organization. Based on my treatment of the analysis of management development needs at the job level (Chapter 5) I would strongly argue that it is not realistic to do this. Recall Sparrow's contention (1994b: 13) that management skills are increasingly organization-specific. Herein may lie the basic flaw in the MCI approach, that universalistic 'standards' of management competence may not be sufficiently specific to provide an organization with a practical enough way of analyzing its management jobs.

In the early 1990s, before developing an organization-specific management competency model, I worked with my team to design and implement a management assessment centre, using MCI standards as criteria. Looking back on the individual reports from those centres now, and comparing them with reports from more recent competency-based assessment centres, I am struck by their relative narrowness and blandness in terms of the development options they identified. At best, the assessment could be considered as trainability testing for individuals who were thinking of attempting the Certificate or Diploma in Management qualifications. This, of course, amounted to circularity, as no systematic attempt was made to predict the effect on the organization of the qualifications themselves. The lesson for us as management developers is that we would do better to concentrate our efforts on the problems of our own organizations than to try and serve some putative 'national interest', which might well divert us from our main priorities. Indeed, we are more likely to serve the national interest precisely by focusing on what we can change within organizations, rather than allowing ourselves to be swept into grandiose ideological initiatives.

Management development as humanism

In Chapter 7, I drew attention to a long and influential humanistic tradition in organization theory. This tradition had numerous antecedents, but a major one was concern about, and reaction against, the Taylorite 'scientific' management creed and, as I have noted earlier, with good reason. I shall not offer a critique of humanism here, but rather draw attention to what can and does happen when it is applied over-zealously to the field of management development. This can be characterized as the triumph of values over sense, and allowing the apparently laudable desire to 'do the right thing' to overrule what is functional to the organization. This is not to suggest that management developers, or anyone else, should not have or display values, particularly ethical ones, nor that they should put aside their values every time it might appear expedient to an organization so to do. But developers do need to be clear about what management development is *for*, why it is that their employers pay them to do the jobs that they do. My contention is that most employers would not see the purpose of management development as 'improving' humanity, specifically that sub-species of humanity we call managers. Nor, I suspect, would most employers set out to *de*humanize managers, though some of them regrettably succeed in doing just that. Most employers make an association between the performance of their managers and the results of their organizations, and infer that there will be some functional advantage to the organization by increasing the level of competence – however they define that – of their managers. If they did not, then arguably management development would not exist.

Yet one can frequently be left with the impression, both by line managers and developers, that management development exists almost for its own sake, and that its value should not be questioned. Furthermore, development is held to be something to which every manager, and indeed every employee, is *entitled*, like the National Health Service or state education. This type of outlook is reflected, for example, in a senior manager's request to a developer to find space at a training programme for a manager who 'could do with a course' because 'it's a long time since he last had one'. For the developer to ask 'in what ways does that manager need to improve his performance?' might, in such circumstances, be regarded as unnecessary or even impertinent; the manager has not received training for some time and 'deserves' it. Sometimes, this misplaced altruism can verge on the absurd, or even become damaging.

In one case, a manager was nominated to attend an assessment centre. The manager concerned did not have a particularly successful track record, and soundings taken in the organization suggested that he was not regarded as having strong future potential. Now, it had already been made clear within the organization that assessment was an expensive process, and one which was very demanding for participants, so the individual responsible for assessment felt it proper to challenge this particular nomination with the nominee's boss. The boss's reaction was one of annoyance at having his judgement questioned, and he insisted that his nominee should attend the assessment centre. The nominee did attend, and was rated objectively, but the conclusion was that he generally showed low levels of competency and would have great difficulty in substantially increasing them, particularly as he was at quite a late stage in his career. A short while after his attending the centre, the manager's job was made redundant and his employment was terminated. On questioning – again – about his decision to nominate this particular manager for assessment, his boss confessed that the termination decision had been taken some time before the assessment centre was due to take place, but he felt that the manager concerned deserved to attend and would still, even having been made redundant, find the feedback useful. The rationale was, it seemed, well-intentioned but one of the consequences was that other managers in the organization began to surmise, reasonably but falsely, that the redundant manager's departure was *as a result of* his attending the assessment centre. This incurred the risk that the event, and the whole process of assessment, would be discredited.

Another manifestation of the humanistic view of development is that entitlement is universal, that a treatment found to be beneficial in one part of the organization should be offered everywhere. Thus if the use of competencies as the basis of assessment has been found beneficial for overcoming succession problems at senior management levels, there is often an inclination to want to extend this process to other categories of employee. It may be that other categories could benefit, but the logic of 'it worked here so it must work there, too' is entirely spurious. Unless needs are identified in the way I have suggested in earlier chapters, there can be no certainty that the success of any given intervention is replicable elsewhere. Unfortunately, this type of mentality can also create 'me-too' demands in organizations. 'If the managers in Production have all had this training, I want it for my managers in Marketing.' This type of thinking is, of course, grist to the mill of those engaged in supply-driven training and development. According to them, everybody would benefit from mentoring, coaching, 360-degree feedback, leadership training in the outdoors, 'stress management', scuba diving . . .

Finally, there appears to have emerged over recent years, certainly in the UK but possibly elsewhere, a 'school' of management developers steeped in an almost evangelical 'service to mankind' outlook, who use a form of language which appears to have come from mysticism via marriage guidance counselling. This 'New Age' patois can be recognized by its frequent use of words like holistic, experiential and renewal. Their favoured prophets seem to be Jung, who gave them (indirectly and, no doubt, unconsciously) the Myers-Briggs Type Indicator, Bandler and Grinder, who gave them 'Neurolinguistic Programming', and the learning organization proselytes, who have given them endless opportunities for reconstruction. Much of the membership of this school appears to be sole trader management training providers. Perhaps they are huddling together for warmth around this cosy metaphysical fire while the cold winds of economic reality blow around them. For all their apparent eclecticism, however, they are nevertheless a fully-equipped phalanx of the supply-driven legion, heavily emphasizing individual development, sometimes to the point of appeals to narcissism. An unsolicited flyer recently received by the author contains some interesting examples of these offerings, inviting the developer to, among other things, 'rediscover the natural grace and posture of children', 'release yourself from habitual patterns of muscular tension and move freely . . .' and, intriguingly, celebrate 'the Spring Equinox with a wild weekend of drumming, dancing and a sweat lodge'. Fascinating and appealing though these individual-level programmes look, I suspect that finding corroborating development needs at organizational and job levels might prove difficult. The management developer may not wish to ignore this type of material completely, but would do well to keep it mentally filed in the 'popular psychology and self-help' category rather than 'organizational change'.

Management development as reward for good behaviour

In Chapter 2 I noted that the *Management Training Directory* (1997) contains 192 references to providers of venues for management training courses. This is but the tip of a very large iceberg. Go to any sizeable hotel in the United Kingdom or United States on any weekday and you are likely to encounter groups of people attending management training courses or conferences. After a heavy day of listening to speakers and occasionally being asked to participate in activities, they may be invited to relax afterwards by having a swim at the hotel pool, or a workout in the gym, before having drinks and a lavish dinner. Later, they may be regaled by one of a growing army of 'motivational' speakers who will invite parallels between climbing Everest or coaching a rowing team (which they have done) with managing a brush factory (which they will never do). These events are now so common that one would have to question how well the 'hospitality' industry would do without them. Some management developers need to exercise care that when booking such events for managers they do not choose venues whose standards fall before the expectations of their eager-to-learn participants. The quality of the golf course, food and wine may be remembered long after whatever learning was supposed to take place has evaporated, and the management developer reminded what a good or bad job s/he did with the arrangements. There may occur an all too insidious association between 'management development' and 'leisure': the idea that when managers are nominated to attend courses, they are being given 'time off for good behaviour'.

When such an association is made, it is likely to reduce development to the level of an inducement or perk. In turn, this may lead to other feelings and behaviours which have nothing to do with development, such as envy and competition between managers to attend more frequent or more attractive programmes. I recall one particularly competitive individual who was not eligible, based on the function he performed, for a particular programme, but regarded the programme as such a prestigious impression management opportunity that he pestered his boss to nominate him for it. The boss eventually and inevitably weakened, and in so doing weakened the whole event, since the individual concerned was not employed, as were other participants, in a substantive management role and was therefore able to contribute little to the proceedings, other than strident advice on the choice of dinner wines and a constant stream of self-serving repartee.

The problem is that if the notion of development as reward takes hold it becomes, like bribery in some countries, accepted as the norm and extremely difficult to shift. Senior managers start bestowing favours which are jockeyed for by their juniors, and management developers start to be seen as intercessors who might be able to 'swing' an individual's nomination to a programme.

Developers may then, perversely, begin to see this as a source of personal power and influence, especially if they have little positional power, and development becomes a Byzantine-like world where learning is, if it is anywhere, at the very bottom of the agenda.

Management development as a propagator of ideology

Abrahamson and Fombrun (1992: 179), in their consideration of how 'organizations participate in shaping the cultural environments of the nations that they inhabit' comment thus: '. . . the corporation school of the 1910s, modern business schools, the MBA, as well as corporate training and development programmes may function not only as instruments of skill-building, but as possible vehicles for the propagation of ideological content'. There are, in my experience, two distinct ways in which management development can act as though it were propagating ideology, first across the population of managers as a whole, and second, within a given organization.

In Chapter 2 I argued that the role of management is difficult to pin down. This has a potential consequence for those occupationally engaged in management, which is that they might suffer if not an identity crisis, at least some misgivings about the validity of their role. Where this occurs, they may well value some bolstering from one source or another (du Gay *et al.*, 1996; Clark and Salaman, 1998), and this bolstering may conveniently be given under the cover of 'management development', for example from being exposed to the thoughts of management 'gurus' or, in other ways, believing that their competence is being enhanced through a training programme. It is interesting that, beyond the original and literal role of the guru as a teacher and spiritual guide to religious adherents, gurus today exist largely for managers, and not for other professionals. If gurus do exist for dentists, geneticists, social scientists, lawyers and architects, they do not tread as broad a world stage, nor command such enormous performance fees, as the management gurus. Whatever the cause of the management gurus' following, anyone who has attended their performances would have no doubt about their capacity to act as carriers of managerialist ideology: lionizing the great contemporary messiahs of management, describing how guru ideas and techniques were applied in raising organizations almost from the dead, prophesying the downfall of those managers and organizations who ignore the signs and portents shown to them. These gurus' brand of evangelism is not conveyed at outdoor prayer rallies but in the comfort of hotel banqueting suites, where the event might have a sub-title such as 'a crucial one-day event on the business strategies that will win in the twenty-first century'. By the end of the event, the participants can return to their organizations with the assurance that they have experienced some personal development, and can prove it by being able to recount to their colleagues a few of the stories which the guru told them. They might also offer to circulate the handouts, or give a short presentation about their day. Thus is ideology propagated, the word made flesh, and the manager's training record and curriculum vitae embellished.

The notion of ideological propagation could apply equally well to development activities within organizations as the transmission of ideas between them. Let us suppose that one of the participants at a conference of the type described above is the chief executive of a large public company. He finds in the guru's words some resonance with ideas he has been having about possible changes within his organization, but whereas he has up until now had some difficulty articulating them, he finds that the guru seems to have the vocabulary to describe them in a plausible and appealing way. Where the chief executive has seen production problems in terms of backlogs and bottlenecks, the guru offers the attractions of a world of 'total quality', where people put aside their individual viewpoints and aspirations in favour of 'teamwork', and production problems melt away. Where the chief executive was concerned about uneven performance and low levels of competence among his managers, the guru offers 'empowerment'; only encourage the managers to 'own the issues of the enterprise' and 'act like coaches' and they will soon start to perform magnificently. And that problem of falling sales? Well, the issue there is one of 'market segmentation' and offering your customers the appropriate 'value proposition'. The chief executive may be tempted to employ external consultants to apply such ideas, and if he does is unlikely to have difficulty in finding them (Czarni-awska-Joerges, 1990).

It is perfectly possible, in management development as in life, to devote a great amount of intellect, energy, time and money to an ideal, with that certainty which only comes from faith – in a deity, in a guru, in human nature – and with no objective evidence either that the source of one's faith is 'right', or that the outcomes promised by that source will materialize. Of all the quackery and chicanery in the world of management development, the ideological variety is the most insidious. Like a debilitating disease, it can quickly and virulently gnaw away at the body, senses and cash of the organization and, once it has taken hold, prove remarkably resilient to any form of attack from managers and management developers alike. The big thing about ideology is that dissent, even in the form of mild scepticism, is usually interpreted as disloyalty and, in an uncertain organizational environment, expressions of dissent may well be career-threatening. Regrettably, this particular 'disease' shows no signs of abating.

Some final reflections

The predominant view I have taken throughout is that management development has an existence as real as most of the phenomena habitually researched by social scientists, and that the most likely explanation for this phenomenon is that it serves some functional purpose for those entities – organizations and individuals – which provide and receive it. Indeed, one of my opening comments was that management development was something that *could* be managed. Throughout the book, we have seen numerous examples of how it can be managed *badly*. There is a common theme underlying the mismanagement of management development, which is that poor management development is badly *grounded*. It pays insufficient attention and analysis to needs. It follows fashion or obeys dogma. Worst of all, it can serve the purveyors of ideas and ideals far more handsomely than the organizations which are paying for them. In its worst excesses, management development could be likened to the scandal of nineteenth-century quack medicine: ungrounded, unregulated, unethical and, above all, ineffective. Is it not time that management started putting its management development house in order?

In this book I have suggested things – ideas, techniques, experiences and caveats – which attempt to pull management development into a conceptually integrated set of questions and methods. I recapitulate the key points in Table 9.1.

Table 9.1 Key concepts in managing management development

Concept	Chapter	Key points
1 Managerial work	2	1.1 Contrast between *pre*scriptive and *de*scriptive approaches. Need to base management development on how managerial work is conceived and operated in one's own organization.
2 Agenda	3	2.1 Management *development* differentiated from management *education* and management *training*. 2.2 *Sensemaking*. What makes sense about management development may vary according to the position and power of 'sensemakers' in the organization. 2.3 *Power*. Is the management development function seen as adding *value* to the organization? Is it helping management cope with uncertainty? Is it difficult to replace?
3 Needs analysis – organization level	4	3.1 Importance of analysing at *organization*, *job* and *individual* levels. 3.2 Different concepts of organization – machine, organism, etc. – lead to different concepts of organizational effectiveness. 3.3 The relevance of management development to various criteria of organizational effectiveness, e.g., *goal attainment* and *open systems*.

Table 9.1 Continued

Concept	Chapter	Key points
4 Needs analysis – job level	5	4.1 Criticality of *job analysis*. Difficulties in analysing managerial jobs. Value of *competency* methodology for this purpose. 4.2 Application of competency models to management development and HR practices – succession planning, recruitment assessment, programme design and evaluation, etc.
5 Needs analysis – individual level	6	5.1 Methods of identifying needs: appraisal; 360-degree feedback; assessment centres.
6 Learning theory	7	6.1 Managers as *adult* learners, and implications for management development. 6.2 Some relevant theories: social learning theory; expectancy theory; goal setting theory; theory of reasoned action; contract theory. 6.3 Questionable rhetoric: *the learning organization*.
7 Selecting, defining, evaluating interventions	8	7.1 Defining what *effectiveness* means in terms of solving a given problem. 7.2 Applying a *research design* approach. 7.3 The model case of Latham and Saari (1979).
8 Alternative perspectives	9	Metaphors of management development as the *professionalization of management*; as *humanism*; as *reward for good behaviour*; as *a propagator of ideology*.

I conclude by asking a number of difficult questions, put to you, the reader. If you have any current responsibility for developing managers because you are a line manager (in which case the responsibility automatically goes with the job), or a human resources executive, or a management developer, you should try to answer them.

Does the set of activities concerned with developing of managers in your organization have a distinctive agenda?

Is management development serving a real and distinctive organizational purpose?

If the answer to these questions is no, the chances are that you are engaged in a game which could be termed 'we do management development here because it's what organizations like ours do'. The chances also are that management development receives little attention or support from your organization's power players, that your focus is on short-term training rather than longer term development and that most of the new ideas about how managers should be trained come from your suppliers, not from you. If, on the other hand, you have thought about and articulated how management development should act as a vehicle for change in helping your organization achieve its goals, you have an agenda. If you have won support from senior management for that agenda, you have power where it matters. If you have an agenda but require greater support from senior management, consider what might make them feel more disposed towards you. What is senior management's agenda and how could you use it to promote yours, specifically by making it 'make sense' to your 'sensemakers'? This may mean probing beneath the surface problems to the deeper and more sensitive ones, such as how succession to the top job(s) is to be handled, how the top team works together, why it is that behaviours espoused for the organization are not actually modelled by senior managers. This can only be done *within* your organization; you are not likely to address these problems by looking outside the organization for models of 'best practice' or 'benchmarks'. However, it is possible that you will need help from outside in the form of skilful process consultation. And it is also possible that you can gain credibility and influence for the management development function by choosing an effective process consultant to help senior management with these problems. There is one slight problem here, which is that really skilful process consultants are few and far between. They tend to work alone or in small associations (perhaps as a sideline to academic work) and not for the large consulting firms, who prefer their consultants to offer customers ready-made 'boiler-plate' solutions. Though the search may be difficult, it will repay the effort.

Have you construed what 'management' really means in your organization?

Have you an effective grasp of what it is in your organization that managers actually *do*?

I have pointed out the limitations of prescription. What managers are supposed to do, according to the writings of the classical school of management theorists and their successors, may bear little resemblance to what managers in your organization really do, or how they are really valued. We have seen time and again how behaviours and values which are espoused as desirable inevitably yield to behaviours and values which are considered to 'work around here'. Some honest introspection could be useful, as could the presence of a well-researched set of managerial competencies. If your role is considered to have some managerial content, think of what norms you share with your management colleagues, and those which you do not.

Let us take again, and for the last time, the age-old problem of appraisal. Suppose that you are a management developer who finds appraisal useful in planning and monitoring objectives for your own subordinates. However, you also find that, although your organization has a policy that an annual appraisal is 'mandatory' for all employees, only 30 per cent actually receive one. What should you do? You could more strongly publicize your 'Conducting Performance Appraisals' course, ask your chief executive to mention the importance of appraisal again in the next edition of the company newspaper, or personally berate your managerial colleagues for not adhering to the policy. I suspect that if you took any of these actions there might, at best, be a very small though temporary increase in the number of appraisals conducted, but that your influence in the organization could be substantially reduced, and for quite some time. The role of 'corporate police-man' is, in my experience, best left to the finance function, not to management development. It would be far more productive for you to consider, or go and find out, what managers in your organization actually do to plan and monitor the work and future development of their staff. It may be that some of them are really quite successful at using devices which do not resemble conventional appraisal, but achieve similar – and maybe better – ends for the employee, the manager and the organization. I recall some work I did on this subject and an interview with a senior manager who had created a very successful operation from an erstwhile mediocre one. During the interview he admitted that he did not carry out formal appraisals, but that individual performance, particularly financial performance, was strongly monitored and much informal feedback given about it. Of development, he said this, which is taken from my interview transcript:

> We've been able to take people and place them in jobs well before they were ready . . . Putting people *in* jobs rather than preparing them. I look for natural leadership, people who are identified as a cut above. People who are articulate, intelligent; people who influence other people. People who convey the image that they have the desire to win and succeed . . . What I bring is the ability to identify someone because they have the raw material to be better than the rest. I reach in and pull them up.

Now the question must be asked that if a manager neglected the formal appraisal process but behaved in the way the manager quoted above described, would individual employee development suffer? Arguably, it would not; individuals given early opportunities to learn by doing may well learn more, and more quickly, than being offered fare from the organization's training manual at the end of each annual appraisal. Interestingly, that particular manager did send his people on formal development programmes where he considered it would be of benefit, and those people inevitably told others that they considered their manager to have a deep concern for their development needs. How powerful it is, in management development terms, when a manager seen as successful models this type of behaviour. The usual, gradualist, 'training' approach pales into insignificance beside it.

*Do you have a systematic approach to the analysis of
management development needs?*

Does this approach differentiate, and ultimately integrate,
organizational, job and individual levels?

At the risk of labouring a point which should by now be very
clear, it is imperative to avoid the trap into which I see many
developers fall, of believing that the organization will improve as
a result of fixing on the improvement of individual managers, 'fill-
ing them up' with lots of knowledge and skills. Certainly, learning
is an individual response; an organization can no more learn, in a
biological sense, than it can breathe, eat and have moods. But
simply to seek to improve the knowledge and skill 'stock' of one's
management in the hope that there will automatically accrue
some benefit to the performance of the organization is a hope-
lessly naïve concept. Unless the learning is grounded in some
genuinely organizational need, then arguably *any* individual
intervention is as good as any other. You don't feel confident?
We'll send you white water rafting. You think you ought to be
more assertive? Here's your personal counsellor. You're badly
organized? Try this time management course. (You'll get a leather-
bound personal organizer at the end.)

Now it is perfectly possible that the senior managers of an
organization have determined, possibly because they have fore-
seen what changes they need and what their managers will have
to do to achieve them, that self-confidence, assertiveness and personal effectiveness need to be generally raised among their
management population. They may also have concluded that
white water rafting, personal counselling and time management
courses are likely to be effective means of achieving the changes
they seek. But this, in my experience, would be the exception
rather than the rule. Needs analysis so often starts and finishes at
the wrong end of the spectrum. As we have seen, it is very much
in the interests of those who supply development on a commodity
basis that this should be so. It is not in the interests of organizations and, strangely, it is often not in the interests of individuals,
either. I suspect I am not alone in having witnessed staff being
made redundant whose training records show page after page of
attendance at short, low-level management training courses.

In the chapters on organizational, job and individual management development needs, I have offered certain techniques for analysing them. These are certainly not the *only* techniques available, as I hope I have made clear. Ultimately, it is not so much the individual techniques that are important as the overall process. However, for those practitioners who are still unsure of the benefits of the competency approach, I trust I may have convinced you of the benefit of exploring it further.

Are you confident that the expertise exists within your organization to align learning interventions with learning needs effectively?

Is there adequate theoretical knowledge about the ways in which individuals can obtain the greatest benefit from a particular learning experience?

The higher up the organization one takes management development, the greater is the risk of getting it wrong in a political, as well as a technical, sense. All managers – indeed, all employees – surely deserve the most appropriate choice of interventions from developers, but to recommend the 'wrong' intervention to a very senior manager might bring the developer, and her team, close to feeling the kiss of death. I have emphasized that, in selecting interventions for managers, it is a case not only of what they are to learn but *how* they are to learn it, and this is associated with their *disposition* towards learning, whether we articulate that as motivation, sense of self-efficacy, 'learning attitude', or use some other description.

Some fortunate management developers may be able to rely on their intuition to consistently find the most appropriate interventions for managers. The rest of us have to rely on science. I have shown how an understanding of learning theory can help us in our choices. I have hardly scratched the surface of learning theory in this book, but hope to have sufficiently demonstrated its importance and utility. This does not mean that all management developers should have a degree in cognitive science, interesting though that prospect might be. But it does mean that developers should be informed by the theories which are available to them. It is, in my view, a healthy sign that an increasing number of people with an occupational psychology qualification and background are being employed by training and development departments, since this is one way of bringing theoretical and empirical knowledge to bear on learning issues.

How do you evaluate the effectiveness of management development in your organization?

How do you know that the money spent on management development is giving you a good return?

There is much to be said for leaving the really difficult questions until last. I have suggested that unless an approach resembling the design of good research is applied to the selection and design of management development, not only will you find it difficult to carry out evaluation, you will not even know what is to be evaluated. I suggest that if you are one of those developers who are trading on past success and your reputation for 'spotting winners', but not particularly concerned about how your work is evaluated, beware. There is no reason why those who run your organization should apply weaker criteria to your effectiveness than they do to, for example, sales people. Why should they not apply the same critical examination to what you propose to invest in management development programmes as they do for production engineers asking them to invest in new plant? There is nothing sacrosanct about management development; several erstwhile management developers, who were unable to prove the value of their function to their organizations, will provide testimony to that. It might be a little dramatic to suggest the slogan *evaluate or die*, but you would do well not to express surprise, and even less, indignation, if you are one day called to account to justify management development activity in your organization. I opened this book with the proposition that, as the title suggests, management development *is* manageable. It is, and the senior management of organizations has every right to expect it to be.

APPENDIX:
ACCESSING AND USING
COMPETENCIES FOR
MANAGEMENT DEVELOPMENT

The research study described here was conducted in a medium-sized international financial services organization, an insurance brokerage business, which at that time employed about 11,500 employees. Slightly less than half the employees were based in the UK, slightly less than half in the US, and the rest dispersed in over 100 offices in other countries around the world. The motive for the study came from a growing recognition within the organization that the reliability of a traditional model for promoting people to senior management positions – to take the most commercially successful entrepreneurs and give them increasing general management responsibilities – was questionable. That 'syndrome of personal characteristics' – using Williams's (1998) terminology – which made for successful performance as an insurance broker was not necessarily that which made for successful performance as a general manager. As Boyatzis (1982: 3) noted, it is not usually the case that 'the best salesperson will make the best sales manager'. This issue was a real and pressing one for the study organization, which was making strenuous efforts to improve its executive succession planning process. According to Hirsh *et al.* (1990), a number of interdependent factors are important in achieving effective outcomes for succession planning:

- a high-level body with the power to make substantive decisions about the type and timing of development interventions for succession candidates;
- an identified 'pool' of candidates considered (by members of the decision-making bodies) to have the potential to succeed to senior posts in the organization;
- accurate biographical data about the candidates, including their development history;
- active interest and involvement by line management in the succession process;
- appropriate development and assessment methods.

This is a useful list. In my experience, all five of these items are genuinely critical to the succession planning. But it is the fifth item, appropriate development and assessment methods, which stands out as having greater significance and complexity than the other four combined. For development and assessment methods to qualify as 'appropriate', they must relate to some notion of succession *criteria.* How might a succession decision be judged as successful after the event? What outcomes should have been attained? The answers to these will depend on what any particular organization requires of its managers, but recall the Schmitt and Klimoski criteria of organizational effectiveness in Chapter 4. It is a logical possibility that if one or more of those criteria were to be required, then the possession and application of certain competencies could be found, over time, to be reliable predictors of an individual's capacity to meet, or at least contribute to the attainment of, organizational criteria. Indeed, if competencies did not have this predictive validity, they would be of little practical use to the organization. They would be no more than groundless pieces of rhetoric, describing aspects of individuals which might be nice to have. As Campbell *et al.* (1970: 10) put it:

> Conclusions about personal characteristics of managers and how they should do their jobs to achieve effective outcomes cannot continue to rest on such flimsy grounds as hunches,

insights by experts, or mere responses to questionnaires . . . I cannot over-emphasize the essential inadequacy of opinions, hunches, speculations and expertise as a basis for prescriptions concerning the predictions of effective executive job behaviour.

So if competencies are to serve a purpose beyond that of the inadequate prescriptions observed by Campbell *et al.* – if they are to be better than fragments of armchair wisdom – they have to be based on research, not invention. It is all too easy to invent competency descriptions which sound plausible to others, or cull them from external sources. The result will usually be a pastiche of descriptions of human qualities with which the inventors may initially be pleased, but later find difficult to operationalize in a way which satisfactorily discriminates between levels of knowledge, skill, ability, self-motivation or any other differences which might account for variation in performance.

It was with this consideration firmly in mind that the research in the study organization was planned. Three objectives were identified for the project:

1 To access constructs of managerial competency which might serve as performance predictors for human resource decisions, especially executive succession planning.
2 To establish, as far as possible, the validity and reliability of these constructs both within the study organization, through triangulation of the results of different access methods, and externally by comparisons with results from other organizations.
3 To ensure that due attention was given to relevant theoretical and empirical studies of managerial effectiveness which might inform the findings and conclusions of the research. (The study therefore included a review of the relevant literature.)

From these objectives, the design of the research was required to accomplish three things. First, a method was needed to develop descriptions of managerial competencies within the study organization. Moreover, it was felt that these descriptions should be obtained using two different methods to see whether these different methods produced significantly different results. Second, it was decided to develop descriptions of certain *non*-managerial competencies within the study organization to see whether they were different from managerial ones. Our concern here was to try to find out whether people's notions of 'management' were different from their general notions of 'senior people', a category which would include employees with very important client relationship responsibilities, or in high-level corporate staff roles. Finally, there was considered some possible value in obtaining a sample of descriptions of managerial competencies obtained from research in other organizations and comparing them against those obtained in the study organization. The rationale for this had a dual aspect: were constructs of managerial competency in the study organization sufficiently close to those in a larger, external sample to indicate consistency with general notions of what managers do, and were there any constructs which appeared unique to the study organization? These requirements suggested that four samples of data should be collected:

1 Constructs of managerial competency from within the study organization, using the repertory grid method (see, e.g., Bramley, 1992: 53–7) to obtain the descriptions.
2 Constructs of senior client relationship competencies relating to insurance broking, again obtained using repertory grid.
3 A second sample of managerial competencies, obtained within the study organization, based on interviews with managers using the critical incident technique (Flanagan, 1954).
4 A third sample of managerial competencies, obtained from published and unpublished studies. This used 17 separate studies as sources, which included data from 22 different organizations, in various industries, plus individual data.

Further details of the samples, and number of constructs identified by method, are given in Figure A.1. Note that there are several possible methods which can be used to access constructs, depending on the circumstances in, and resources available to, the study organization. The reader is referred to the work of Kandola and Pearn (1992) for descriptions of these.

The content of each of the four samples was analysed, and common or similar descriptions were clustered into 36 categories. For each pair of samples, frequencies of construct citation were

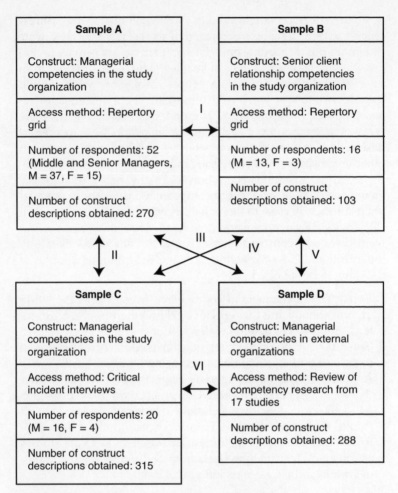

Figure A.1 Data samples, attributes and relationships
Note: The four samples, A–D, provide six opportunities for comparison between them, I–VI.

ranked and correlation coefficients (Spearman's *rho*) calculated. The results were as shown in Table A.1.

These findings show that managerial competencies in the study organization (Samples A and C) did not correlate strongly with senior client relationship competencies, nor were these

Appendix

Table 1 Inter-sample correlations

SAMPLE	A Managerial competencies in study organization, accessed by repertory grid	B Senior client relationship competencies in study organization accessed by repertory grid	C Managerial competencies in study organization, accessed by critical incident interview
B	0.079		
C	0.559**	−0.027	
D	0.396*	0.240	0.413*
Managerial competencies in external organizations			

* $p < 0.05$
** $p < 0.01$

correlations significant. For management competencies accessed by the critical incident method, the correlation with senior client relationship competencies was negative. However, there was strong and very significant correlation between internal constructs of managerial competency obtained using different access methods. Finally, there was moderate but significant correlation between external constructs of managerial competency (Sample D) and the two internal samples (A and C) of managerial competency. The findings therefore tended to support the study hypotheses, that:

1 Constructs of managerial roles within the study organization would be appreciably different from constructs of other senior but non-managerial roles, i.e. those of senior brokers.
2 Competencies identified for managerial roles within the study organization would resemble those described for a range of other organizations.
3 Constructs of managerial roles within the study organization would be held consistently, regardless of the method by which they were accessed.

Although the study inevitably had its limitations, particularly with regard to the size of the sample of internal respondents, it nevertheless tended to support competency assessment as a practical and reliable means of job analysis for managerial work. It identified the main job requirements individuals were perceived to have in order to perform effectively as a manager. The preliminary competency model obtained for the study organization is shown as Table A.2. It will perhaps contain few surprises, as construing takes place in a social setting and the descriptions are as much about what respondents think managers *should* do as what managers actually do. One major difference between this

Table 2 Constructs of managerial competency in the study organization

Primary competencies	*Related competency descriptions*
1 Involving, consulting, seeking participation from, staff	1.1 Outgoing approach
2 Acting with honesty, sincerity and fairness	2.1 Behaving consistently and persistently
	2.2 Emotionally stable
3 Acting decisively, 'leading from the front'	3.1 Commanding respect
	3.2 Leading by example
	3.3 Conscientious
	3.4 Having good knowledge of role and task
4 Promoting needs of, supporting, caring for, subordinates	4.1 Giving counselling, coaching, training
5 Showing capacity and willingness to delegate	5.1 Experimenting
6 Communicating clearly; giving direction concisely	6.1 Briefing staff frequently, regularly, systematically
	6.2 Listening attentively; actively seeking feedback
7 Planning, strategizing, conceptualizing a vision	7.1 Able to inspire others by creating and articulating a vision
	7.2 Thinking creatively and innovatively
8 Sensing and solving problems	8.1 Using rationality in decision making

model and that for most other organizations, however, was the salience of 'honesty, sincerity and fairness' in the minds of members of the study organization.

Having developed such a model, and perhaps given some comfort to those people in the study organization who commissioned the research that notions of management are internally consistent, generally consistent with external notions and distinctively different from notions of other senior professional roles, the question then arises: 'and so what?' How could such a model be utilized as a tool for management succession planning and development? Let us examine this particular case, and what subsequently happened in the study organization following development of the model.

First, agreement was reached with the chief executive and top management team that the approach to succession planning should follow the following process:

1 *Selection of a pool of high-performing candidates considered to have the potential to succeed to the most senior management jobs in the organization.* Each member of the executive committee (the directors with the line responsibility for the organization's business units) was asked to nominate those individuals considered to have the potential to perform executive committee-level roles in a five- to ten-year timescale. This generated a cadre of about 120 nominees.

2 *Evaluation of the development needs of the 120 nominees through individual assessment, using the competency model as the basis for designing performance predictors.* The descriptions from the model were operationalized so as to produce a five-point Behaviourally Anchored Rating Scale (BARS) for *each* of the competencies. For example, for the competency concerned with promoting the needs of, supporting and caring for subordinates – abbreviated to *developing others* – the scale was:

0 Competency not observed.
1 Focuses on strengths and areas for development, e.g., makes objective strengths and development needs on the basis of tangible evidence.
2 Provides practical support, e.g., makes time to coach and help others to learn.
3 Gives constructive feedback for development, e.g., identifies

individual strengths and weaknesses and gives specific, timely feedback.

4 Creates long-term development opportunities, e.g., arranges appropriate projects or assignments to facilitate others' long-term development.

An assessment centre was then designed; a battery of tests and exercises was developed with the object of allowing those being assessed to demonstrate each competency, and a group of observers was trained to identify accurately the point on the rating scale at which each competency was demonstrated. All the nominees were assessed, using this method, over a three-year period. For each nominee the outcomes were, first and obviously, the assessment itself, but also, crucially, the assessors' judgements about nominees' major development needs, recommendations on how those needs could be met through various interventions, and agreement of a development plan between the nominee and his or her top management sponsor. The top management team then committed to review collectively the progress of each nominee against the plan every six months, and that process continues.

3 *Modification or replacement of existing management training programmes so as to ground their learning objectives and design in the management competency model.* For example, a programme which had been developed and run for senior executives based on the rather loose objectives of improving their problem-solving and decision-making abilities was reconstructed around those competency descriptions most closely associated with those abilities. One effect of this was that those charged with teaching this programme were able to define learning outcomes more closely, and create more rigorous hypotheses about what learning methods and materials would more likely enable those outcomes to be achieved. This in turn allowed a more rigorous evaluation process to be devised for the programme (see Chapter 8).

4 *Development of multi-rater (or '360-degree') feedback instruments, grounded in the competency descriptions, as a means of diagnosing individual development needs.* This approach was examined in depth in Chapter 6.

5 *Basing the recruitment and selection of new managers substantially on competency predictors.* As Herriot observes (1989: 433), 'most interviews are poor selection tools' because most selection interviews are unstructured. But he points out that when selection interviews are based on a standardized format and on job analysis – when they are *structured* and *situational* – their reliability and validity in predicting the future performance of interviewees are greatly improved. He cites research studies which obtained predictive validity coefficients of 0.41 and 0.45 through the use of structured interviews, whereas the validity coefficient for unstructured interviews rarely rises above 0.20. In the case of the study organization, the recruitment method, initially for senior positions but ultimately for all managerial and professional jobs, is being changed to include structured interviews, based on the competency models. So, for example, where the competency of conceptualizing strategy is being sought, the question to candidates might be: 'Could you tell me about a time you recognized that a significant change to your business was needed, and what you did about it?' From the responses given (and, where necessary, challenged by the interviewer) it is possible not only to assess the candidate's level of competency, but also to judge the relevance of the context in which the candidate sets his or her narrative. It would be very interesting to know how implementing these methods is improving the validity of selection in the study organization. At the time of writing, however, the start of the change of method is very recent and, alas (and perhaps typically of most organizations), no past data had ever been collected on the validity of unstructured interviewing methods.

REFERENCES

Abrahamson, E. and Fombrun, C.J. (1992) Forging the iron cage: Inter-organizational networks and the production of macro-culture, *Journal of Management Studies*, 29(2), 175–94.

Ajzen, I. (1991) The theory of planned behaviour, *Organizational Behaviour and Human Decision Processes*, 50, 179–211.

Ajzen, I. and Fishbein, M. (1980) *Understanding Attitudes and Predicting Social Behaviour*. Englewood Cliffs, NJ: Prentice-Hall.

Alvesson, M. (1993) Organizations as rhetoric: Knowledge-intensive firms and the struggle with ambiguity, *Journal of Management Studies*, 30(6), 997–1016.

Amabile, T.M., Conti, R., Coon, H. *et al.* (1993) Work environment differences between high creativity and low creativity projects, in S.S. Gryskiewicz (ed.) *Discovering Creativity*. Greensboro, NC: Centre for Creative Leadership.

Antonacopolou, E.P. and Fitzgerald, L. (1996) Reframing competency in management development, *Human Resource Management Journal*, 6(1), 27–48.

Argyris, C. (1962) *Interpersonal Competence and Organizational Effectiveness*. London: Tavistock.

Argyris, C. (1970) *Understanding Organizational Behaviour*. Homewood, IL.: Dorsey.

Argyris, C. (1990) *Overcoming Organizational Defenses*. London: Allyn and Bacon.

References

Argyris, C. (1992) A leadership dilemma: Skilled incompetence, in G. Salaman (ed.) *Human Resource Strategies*. London: Sage.

Armstrong, P. (1991) Human resource management and changes in management control systems, in J. Storey (ed.) *New Perspectives in Human Resource Management*. London: Routledge.

Asch, S.E. (1962) *Social Psychology*. Englewood Cliffs, NJ: Prentice-Hall.

Bagozzi, R.P. and Kimmel, S.K. (1995) A comparison of leading theories for the prediction of goal-directed behaviours, *British Journal of Social Psychology*, 34(4), 437–61.

Baldwin, T.T. and Ford, J.K. (1988) Transfer of training: A review and directions for further research, *Personnel Psychology*, 41, 63–105.

Baldwin, T.T. and Padgett, M.Y. (1994) Management development: A review and commentary, in C.L. Cooper and I.T. Robertson (eds) *Key Reviews in Managerial Psychology*. Chichester: Wiley.

Bandura, A. (1977a) *Social Learning Theory*. Englewood Cliffs, NJ: Prentice-Hall.

Bandura, A. (1977b) Self-efficacy: Toward a unifying theory of behavioural change, *Psychological Review*, 84(2), 191–215.

Beer, M. (1989) The politics of OD, in W.L French, C.H. Bell. and R.A. Zawacki (eds) *Organization Development: Theory, Practice and Research*. Homewood, IL: BPI Irwin.

Bernardin, H.J. (1996) Subordinate appraisal: A valuable source of information about managers, *Human Resource Management*, 25(3), 421–39.

Bloomfield, B.P. and Vurdubakis, T. (1996) What a performance: Ambiguities of management consultancy as a knowledge practice. Paper presented to The Open University conference on management consultants, September.

Boam, R. and Sparrow, P. (1992) The rise and rationale of competency-based approaches, in R. Boam and P. Sparrow (eds) *Designing and Achieving Competency*. London: McGraw-Hill.

Boyatzis, R.E. (1982) *The Competent Manager*. New York, NY: Wiley.

Bramley, P. (1992) *Evaluating Training Effectiveness*. Maidenhead: McGraw-Hill.

Branscombe, N.R., N'gbala, A., Kobrynowicz, D. and Wann, D.L. (1997) Self and group position concerns influence attributions but they are not determinants of counterfactual mutation focus, *British Journal of Social Psychology*, 36(4), 387–404.

Brown, H. (1985) *People, Groups and Society*. Milton Keynes: Open University Press.

Burke, M.J. and Day, R.R. (1986) A cumulative study of the effectiveness of managerial training, *Journal of Applied Occupational Psychology*, 71, 232–46.

Burns, T. (1990) Mechanistic and organismic structures, in D.S. Pugh (ed.) *Organization Theory.* Harmondworth: Penguin.

Burns, T. and Stalker, G.M. (1961) *The Management of Innovation.* London: Tavistock.

Burrell, G. and Morgan, G. (1979) *Sociological Paradigms and Organizational Analysis.* Aldershot: Gower.

Campbell, J.P., Dunnette, M.D., Lawler, E.E and Weick, K.E. (1970) *Managerial Behaviour, Performance and Effectiveness.* New York, NY: McGraw-Hill.

Carroll, S.J. and Gillen, D.J. (1987) Are the classical management functions useful in describing management work? *Academy of Management Review,* 12(1), 38–51.

Cascio, W. (1991) *Applied Psychology in Personnel Management.* Englewood Cliffs, NJ: Prentice-Hall.

Chandler, A.D. (1990) Managerial hierarchies, in D.S. Pugh (ed.) *Organization Theory.* Harmondsworth: Penguin.

Clark, T. and Salaman, G. (1996) The management guru as organizational witch-doctor, *Organization,* 3(1), 85–107.

Clark, T. and Salaman, G. (1998) Telling tales: Management gurus' narratives and the construction of managerial identity, *Journal of Management Studies,* 35(2), 137–61.

Cobb, R.T. and Margulies, N. (1989) Organization development: A political perspective, in W.L French, C.H. Bell. and R.A. Zawacki (eds) *Organization Development: Theory, Practice and Research.* Homewood, IL: BPI Irwin.

Cockerill, A. (1989) The kind of competence for rapid change, *Personnel Management,* November, 52–6.

Constable, J. and McCormick, R. (1987) *The Making of British Managers.* London: BIM and CBI.

Coopey, J. (1995) Managerial culture and the stillbirth of organizational commitment, *Human Resource Management Journal,* 5(3), 56–76.

Czarniawska-Joerges, B. (1990) Merchants of meaning: Management consulting in the Swedish public sector, in B.A. Turner (ed.) *Organizational Symbolism.* New York, NY: Walter de Gruyter.

Du Gay, P., Salaman, G. and Rees, B. (1996) The conduct of management and the management of conduct: Contemporary managerial discourse and the constitution of the 'competent manager', *Journal of Management Studies,* 33(3), 263–82.

Dulewicz, V. and Fletcher, C. (1992) The context and dynamics of performance appraisal, in P. Herriot (ed.) *Assessment and Selection in Organizations.* Chichester: Wiley.

Employment Department (1990) *Training Statistics 1990.* London: HMSO.

Evans, C. (1978) *Psychology: A Dictionary of the Mind, Brain and Behaviour.* London: Arrow.

Evans, S., Ewing, K. and Nolan, P. (1992) Industrial relations and the British economy in the 1990s: Mrs. Thatcher's legacy, *Journal of Management Studies*, 29(5), 571–89.

Fayol, H. (1949) *General and Industrial Management*. London: Pitman.

Fayol, H. (1990) General principles of management, in D.S. Pugh (ed.) *Organization Theory*. Harmondsworth: Penguin.

Feltham, R.T. (1992) Assessment centres, in P. Herriot (ed.) *Assessment and Selection in Organizations*. Chichester: Wiley.

Fiedler, F.E. (1990) Situational control and a dynamic theory of leadership, in D.S. Pugh (ed.) *Organization Theory*. Harmondsworth: Penguin.

Flanagan, J.C. (1954) The critical incident technique, *Psychological Bulletin*, 51(4), 327–58.

Fletcher, C., Baldry, C. and Cunningham-Snell, N. (1998). Psychometric properties of alternative performance appraisal systems. Paper presented to the British Psychological Society Occupational Psychology conference, Eastbourne, January.

Fletcher, C. and Williams, R.S. (1992) *Performance Appraisal and Career Development*. Cheltenham: Stanley Thornes.

French, W.L, Bell, C.H. and Zawacki, R.A. (1989) *Organization Development: Theory, Practice and Research*. Homewood, IL: BPI Irwin.

Geis, F.L. and Christie, R. (1970) Overview of experimental research, in R. Christie and F.L. Geis (eds) *Studies in Machiavellianism*. New York: Academic Press.

Gill, J. and Whittle, S. (1993) Management by panacea: Accounting for transience, *Journal of Management Studies*, 30(2), 291–8.

Goffman, E. (1990) *The Presentation of Self in Everyday Life*. Harmondsworth: Penguin.

Goldstein, I.L. (1986) *Training in Organizations*. Pacific Grove, CA: Brooks/Cole.

Goldstein, A.P. and Sorcher, M. (1974) *Changing Supervisory Behaviour*. New York, NY: Pergamon Press.

Gowler, D. and Legge, K. (1991) Rhetoric in bureaucratic careers: Managing the meaning of management success, in M.B. Arthur, D.T. Hall and B.S. Lawrence (eds) *Handbook of Career Theory*. Cambridge: Cambridge University Press.

Greuter, M.A. and Algera, J.A. (1992) Criterion development and job analysis, in P. Herriot (ed.) *Assessment and Selection in Organizations*. Chichester: Wiley.

Grey, C. and French, R. (1996) Rethinking management education: An introduction, in R. French and C. Grey (eds) *Rethinking Management Education*. London: Sage.

Guba, E.G. and Lincoln, Y.S. (1989) *Fourth Generation Evaluation*. Newbury Park, CA: Sage.

Guest, D. (1992) Right enough to be dangerously wrong: An analysis of the *In Search of Excellence* phenomenon, in G. Salaman (ed.) *Human Resource Strategies*. London: Sage.

Guion, R.M. (1989) Comments on personnel selection methods, in M. Smith and I. Robertson (eds) *Advances in Selection and Assessment*. Chichester: Wiley.

Hales, C.P. (1986) What do managers do? A critical review of the evidence, *Journal of Management Studies*, 23(1), 88–115.

Hammer, M. and Champy, J. (1993) *Reengineering the Corporation: A Manifesto for Business Revolution*. London: Nicholas Brearley.

Handy, C. (1987) *The Making of British Managers*. London: NEDO.

Handy, L., Holton, V. and Wilson, A. (1996) Management development, *Training Officer*, 32(5), 140–2.

Hazucha, J.F., Hezlett, S.A. and Schneider, R.J. (1993) The impact of 360-degree feedback on management skills development, *Human Resource Management*, 32(2 & 3), 325–51.

Herriot, P. (1989) The selection interview, in P. Herriot (ed.) *Assessment and Selection in Organizations*. Chichester: Wiley.

Herriot, P. and Pemberton, C. (1995) *New Deals: The Revolution in Managerial Careers*. Chichester: Wiley.

Hinings, C.R., Hickson, D.J., Pennings, J.M. and Schneck, R.E. (1974) A strategic contingency theory of inter-organizational power, *Administrative Science Quarterly*, 19, 216–27.

Hirsh, W., King, G., Lovery, J., Fryatt, J. and Hayday, S. (1990) *Succession Planning: Current Practice and Future Issues*. Brighton: Institute of Manpower Studies.

Hofstede, G. (1990) Motivation, leadership and organization. Do American theories apply abroad?, in D.S. Pugh (ed.) *Organization Theory*. Harmondsworth: Penguin.

Holding, D.H. (1991) Transfer of training, in J.E. Morrison (ed.) *Training for Performance*. Chichester: Wiley.

Honey, P. and Mumford, A. (1995) *Using Your Learning Styles*. Maidenhead: Peter Honey.

Huczynski, A. (1983) *Encyclopaedia of Management Development Methods*. Aldershot: Gower.

Huczynski, A. (1987) *Encyclopaedia of Organizational Change Methods*. Aldershot: Gower.

Hussey, D.E. (1985) Implementing corporate strategy: Using management education and training, *Long Range Plan*, 18(5), 28–37.

IDS (Income Data Services) (1995) Assessing 360-degree appraisal. *IDS Management Pay Review*, 175, 3–8. London: Income Data Services Ltd.

Institute of Management Research Board (1995) *Management Development to the Millennium: The New Priorities*. Corby: Institute of Management.

References

Vicere, A.A., Taylor, M.W. and Freeman, V.T. (1994) Executive development in major corporations: A ten-year study, *Journal of Management Development*, 13(1), 4–22.

Vroom, V.H. (1964) *Work and Motivation*. New York, NY: Wiley.

Walton, R.E. (1989) Interpersonal confrontations and basic third-party functions: A case study, in W.L French, C.H. Bell. and R.A. Zawacki (eds) *Organization Development: Theory, Practice and Research*. Homewood, IL: BPI Irwin.

Warr, P. (1994) *Training for Managers*. Corby: Institute of Management.

Watson, T.J. (1994) Management 'flavours of the month': Their role in managers' lives, *International Journal of Human Resources Management*, 29(1), 73–94.

Weber, M. (1990) Legitimate authority and bureaucracy, in D.S. Pugh (ed.) *Organization Theory*. Harmondsworth: Penguin.

Weick, K.E. (1993) The collapse of sensemaking in organizations: The Mann Gulch Disaster, *Administrative Science Quarterly*, 38(4), 628–53.

Weick, K.E. (1995) *Sensemaking in Organizations*. Thousand Oaks, CA: Sage.

Weston, J.F. and Brigham, E.F. (1982) *Essentials of Managerial Finance*. Chicago, IL: Dryden.

Whitely, W. (1985) Managerial work behaviour: An integration of results from two major approaches, *Academy of Management Journal*, 28, 344–62.

Wiersema, M.F. (1992) Strategic consequences of executive succession within diversified firms, *Journal of Management Studies*, 29(1), 73–94.

Williams, R.S. (1998) *Performance Management: Perspectives on Employee Performance*. London: International Thomson Business Press.

Witkowski, T. and Stiensmeier-Pelster, J. (1998) Performance deficits following failure: Learned helplessness or self-esteem protection? *British Journal of Social Psychology*, 37(1), 59–72.

Wolfe, R.A. (1994) Organizational innovation: Review, critique and suggested research directions, *Journal of Management Studies*, 31(3), 405–31.

Woodruffe, C. (1992) What is meant by a competency?, in R. Boam and P. Sparrow (eds) *Designing and Achieving Competency*. Maidenhead: McGraw-Hill.

Woodward, J. (1958) *Management and Technology*. London: HMSO.

Zaleznik, A. (1992) Managers and leaders: Are they different? *Harvard Business Review*, March–April, 126–35.

Zimbardo, P. and Ebbesen, E.B. (1969) *Influencing Attitudes and Changing Behaviour*. Reading, MA: Addison-Wesley.

INDEX

Index

within political system, 28–9
wide-ranging process, 27
theories
of organization, 36
and rhetoric, 99
of work behaviour, 15
theories-in-use, 24–5, 85
theory of planned behaviour, 93
theory of reasoned action, 83,
92–5, 97, 131
top team
changing behaviour of, 46–7
modelling behaviour, 46, 132
see also executives, senior
total quality management, 10, 16
training
of appraisers, 64
of assessment centre observers,
75–6
for assessment feedback, 73
and development, 22–3, 27, 58–9
evaluation of programmes, 114
expenditure on, 11, 12
focus of, 21–2
industrial, 81
as industry, 11
managers' attitudes to, 34–5
outcome, and variables, 15, 16
and performance management,
85
quick fix, 44
selecting methods, 107
short-term, 132
supply-driven, 102–3, 109, 124,
125, 132
take-up, 11–12, 103
top-down, 34, 85
Training and Enterprise Councils
(TECs), 120

transfer, 109–10
of knowledge, 107–8

uncertainty
coping with, 29–30
of managerial work, 13, 101–2
under-performance, 42, 44

valence, instrumentality and
expectancy (VIE) theory,
88
values
humanist, 122
among managers, 133
variability, in jobs, 52, 55
variables
and individual needs
identification, 60–1
and measurement of
intervention results, 112–13
and training outcome, 15, 16
Vroom, V.H., 88

Warr, P., 11–12
Weick, K.E., 25, 26, 40
Weston, J.F. and Brigham, E.F., 24
Williams, R.S., 55, 138
work
of managers, 130
defining, 120
identifying, 8–9, 12
research, into, 8, 9
uncertainty of, 13, 101–2
see also job analysis
necessary/valued, 29

Zaleznik, A., 17–19
Zimbardo, P. and Ebbesen, E.B.,
49, 50

167